HOMEWARD BOUND

*Building an attractive,
Christ-centered family
on
eternal principles*

EDWARD A. HARTMAN

CHRISTIAN
FOCUS

Edward A. Hartman (B.S., Columbia Bible College; M.Div., Reformed Theological Seminary; D.Min., Westminster Seminary California) served as the senior pastor of First Presbyterian Church (PCA) in Kosciusko, Mississippi for 10 years. In 2005, the Hartman family moved to Brasov, Romania where Ed directs the church planting ministry of Mission to the World in Romania.

ISBN 1-84550-348-1
ISBN 978-1-84550-348-2

© Edward A. Hartman

10 9 8 7 6 5 4 3 2 1

First published in 2001
Reprinted in 2008
by
Christian Focus Publications, Ltd.,
Geanies House, Fearn, Ross-shire,
IV20 1TW, Great Britain.

www.christianfocus.com

Cover design by Moose77.com

Printed by CPD Wales

Would anyone have chosen to endure the ordeal that qualified Ed Hartman to write this extraordinary book? Yet Dr. Hartman was chosen by God for the agony and ecstasy that produced the heart-searching blend of sound theology, pastoral compassion, loving boldness, and personal testimony that you will read in these pages. If you have envied the Puritans' spiritual intimacy with God and equilibrium in adversity but have stumbled over their complex language, Pastor Hartman will introduce you to their insights with clarity and warmth. If the death of a loved one has embittered you against God, planting doubts about his goodness, power, and providence, you need to see the big picture that Dr. Hartman discovered from Solomon, through Perkins: 'The day of death is better than the day that one is born' – really better! The Hartman family has experienced this truth because their life in covenant with the God of grace had been preparing them to 'die well' long before death loomed on the horizon. If your heart thirsts not for pious platitudes from the complacent but for real comfort from a brother who has found God faithful in the valley of death's shadow, read this book.

Dennis E. Johnson
Professor of Practical Theology,
Westminster Seminary, Escondido, California

For the Christian the best is always yet to be. Ed Hartman reminds us of this in a way that comforts, challenges and inspires. Here is a book that shakes the Christian's earthbound preoccupations and turns our hearts toward our ultimate home. I commend it warmly.

Alistair Begg
Senior Pastor,
Parkside Church, Chagrin Falls, Ohio

CONTENTS

INTRODUCTION

In August of 1993, I kissed my wife and children goodbye, drove to the airport and departed for a month of studies toward a Doctor of Ministry degree at Westminster Theological Seminary in California. My interest as a pastor lay first in the effective proclamation of God's inspired, inerrant, infallible Word, and I eagerly looked forward to being sharpened toward that end as I learned from some truly gifted preachers and theologians.

My secondary interest lay in the establishment and maintenance of a godly home, for over my years of ministry I had discovered that few things more attractively display and persuasively commend the glory of God in the life of a Christian than a Christ-centered marriage and the Christ-centered family relationships that grow out of that marriage. God designed the family, in part, to serve as a multi-faceted illustration of the relationship between himself and his people – one that would cause the watching world to sit up and take notice.

How disturbing, then, that the glory of God is so dimly reflected in so many of the families that claim the name of Christ. J. I. Packer has written that we live in 'an era when marriage, even among Christians is becoming brittle and unstable, and serial marriage through a series of divorces is modeled under limelight, so to speak, by top stars in the entertainment world, and casual sexual relations between adults raise no eyebrows, and teenage fornication is shrugged off as a universal and inevitable fact of life, and most children in most homes grow up in pagan ignorance of God and his law.' Packer's immediate answer to this dilemma is, 'there is much to be learned by tracking Puritan thought on marriage and the family.'[1]

So, taking Packer's lead, I set out on a study of what the Puritans had to say about the establishment of a godly marriage and home. I quickly discovered that most of their writing was primarily proactive in nature, in glaring contrast to the reactive or corrective nature of most of today's writing on marriage and the family. I also discovered that rather than simply emphasizing the right behavior necessary in a godly marriage and home, much of their writing went directly to the condition of the heart that prompted and constrained that behavior.

Then in August of 1995, I returned to Westminster for more concentrated study, this time having the privilege of studying the theology of Jonathan Edwards with Dr. John Gerstner. That week marked, in an ominous way, the introduction to the watershed year of my life. On the Saturday of that week, I was studying a number of out-of-print Puritan works on microfilm, when I stumbled across an unusually titled treatise by William Perkins, published in 1616, at the University of Cambridge, *A Salve for a Sicke Man, or A Treatise Containing the Nature, Differences, and Kindes of Death; as also The Right Manner of Dying Well.* The promotional also read, 'it may serve for spiritual instruction to (1) Mariners when they goe to Sea; (2) Soldiers when they goe to Battell; (3) Women when they travell (travail) with childe.' The remainder of the work was specifically titled at the heading of each page, *The Right Way of Dying Well.*

I was so intrigued by this title that I printed all the pages of barely legible text from the microfilm viewer, to be carefully read later. As I put those pages into a folder, I glanced at my watch and noticed that my family was in all likelihood eating breakfast, so I picked up the telephone and dialed our home number. The voice that answered was unexpected, though not unfamiliar. It was one of the girls from our church's high school youth group, who with an uncertain voice informed me that the headaches my wife had been battling for the past several weeks had grown much worse, to the point of her having to be sedated because of the

---

[1] Packer, J. I., *A Quest for Godliness: The Puritan Vision of the Christian Life* (Wheaton: Crossway Books, 1990), p. 270.

now unmanageable pain. The children had been sent to stay with friends, and my wife's mother was on her way to our home to help in any way she could. I was advised that the doctor felt I needed to take the next flight home. He had used the words 'possible brain tumor'.

It was to the pages of William Perkins' treatise, *The Right Way of Dying Well,* that my attention was drawn when, less than two hours later, I sat on an aeroplane flying back to our home in Mississippi. I wrestled deeply on that long flight from San Diego to Dallas, and then on to Jackson. 'This can't be!' were the words that kept running through my mind. My family is supposed to be immune to this kind of crisis. Cancer happens to other families, but certainly not ours! But the title of Perkins' work rang in my ears, and its content played like a film in the theater of my mind.

I was bombarded with reminders of what had become one of my driving convictions: few things more attractively display and persuasively commend the glory of God in the life of a Christian than a Christ-centered marriage and a Christ-centered family ... *one that would cause the watching world to sit up and take notice.* I now desperately wanted to reject the truth that had begun whispering in my mind: sometimes the glory of God is displayed most attractively and commended most persuasively through the *death* of one in a Christ-centered marriage or family.

The watershed year of my life had begun.

A few days later, I was sitting alone on the edge of the bed in an empty hospital room on the fourth floor of the University of Mississippi Medical Center. A neurosurgeon walked in wearing a rumpled set of surgical scrubs, fatigue unmistakably evident in his face. Just a few hours earlier, my wife had been wheeled down to the surgical suites to undergo a biopsy on a fist-sized brain tumor. The neurosurgeon took a seat opposite the bed, sighed deeply, and looked at me as if waiting for me to ask the question. 'How'd it go?' I asked. He took a long, deep breath and said, 'Not as well as we had hoped. The tumor is far more virulent than we had expected and is definitely inoperable.' He paused, and again, just stared, his agony in telling me these things unmistakable. I quietly asked the only question that seemed to follow from his response: 'Is she terminal?' Another long, deep breath – then he quietly said, 'I'm sorry.' My mind began reeling, as all the questions I desperately wanted to ask screamed in my mind. Yet all I could manage was the question he had already answered, 'Are you telling me I'm about to lose my wife?' Again he softly replied, 'I am so sorry. We will do all we can for her.' And with few more words, he stood, put his hand on my shoulder, and left the room. Again, the reminder, *sometimes the glory of God is displayed most attractively and commended most persuasively through the death of one in a Christ-centered marriage or family.*

In God's providence, it was William Perkins, whom J. I. Packer calls 'the C. S. Lewis of the Puritans', who helped me see most clearly that Christ-centeredness in a godly family grows out of living constantly *with a long view*. A perspective that holds in constant view the unshakable reality of eternity as the backdrop to every issue, every relationship, every hope, every dream, every joy, every sorrow, every smile, and every tear. I've learned that as the spiritual head of my marriage and family, I can offer no greater gift to those I hold dear in this life, than to point them constantly to eternity, and to the One who sovereignly rules over it.

In Romans 12:1-2, the apostle Paul challenges us: 'Therefore, I urge you, brothers, in view of God's mercy, to offer your bodies as living sacrifices, holy and pleasing to God – this is your spiritual act of worship. Do not conform any longer to the pattern of this world, but be transformed by the renewing of your mind. *Then you will be able to test and approve what God's will is – his good, pleasing and perfect will.*' It is this 'godly preoccupation' with eternity that lies at the heart of offering our bodies as living sacrifices, and consequently, at the heart of a life of worship. The result of this preoccupation with eternity, Paul tells us, is that we will be able test and approve what God's good, perfect, and pleasing will is. This doesn't simply point to the right *identifying of* or *thinking about* God's will, but it leads us to the right *valuing* of those things that count for eternity. And when we learn to treasure above all else the perfect and pleasing will of God and learn to be satisfied in all that God is for us and offers to us, then everything else in our lives, *and in our families*, regains proper perspective and proportion.

I recognize that for many, the connection between the subjects of 'the godly home' and 'preparing to die well' is not immediately obvious. But I've come to see that the two are inextricably linked. Several months before Amy died, she stopped by the local florist's shop on her way to visit a friend. While she was there, she noticed several large arrangements that had been prepared for a funeral scheduled for later that day. Though the flowers were beautiful, she frowned at the various cards attached to each arrangement. They read, 'With deepest sympathy,' or 'With our condolences.' She slowly shook her head and said to the florist, 'Those cards are far too depressing. I don't want any like those on the flowers at my funeral.' She began thumbing through the cards that were on display, and smiled as she pulled one out and laid it on the counter. 'This is the card I want on my flowers,' she said as she turned and left the shop. Three months later, at her memorial service, all the flowers at the graveside and church included the card she had selected, 'Welcome to your new home.'

I've carried one of those cards with me for quite some time. It serves as a reminder that no matter how comfortable or content I am, this world, and all that it offers, is not my permanent home. But neither is it merely a *temporary* home, with no understanding or expectation of a future one. In the clearest sense, this life is *transitional*, meaning that it is where I now joyfully and gratefully reside, yet with an ever-present expectation of being prepared for that final day when I am welcomed to my new home in heaven. The transitional character of this life is what reminds us to hold in tension the reality of where we are now, and where we will one day be. The apostle John puts it this way: 'How great is the love the Father has lavished on us, that we should be called children of God! And that is what we are (the reality and privilege of where we are now)! The reason the world does not know us is that it did not know him. Dear friends, now we are children of God, and what we will be has not yet been made known. But we know that when he appears, we shall be like him, for we shall see him as he is (the expectation of where we will one day be). Everyone who has this hope in him purifies himself, just as he is pure (the challenge to live in the tension between the two realities)' (1 John 3:1-3).

We live in a consumer culture that exalts and commends living with a passion for the moment. The advertising that relentlessly bombards us depends on that fact. The prospect of future gain is easily set aside in exchange for the personal gratification that is rarely delayed. Consumer debt in our country is at an all-time high, largely because we've bought into the subtle lie that no day of final accounting will arrive, assuming that it can be postponed indefinitely through further indebtedness. Is it any wonder that in this environment the raising of godly families has become increasingly challenging? Our children are not living with an eternal perspective because they have not seen eternity in their own parent's eyes. Nor, more practically, have they seen eternity consistently displayed in their own parents' spending patterns.

Moses reminds us in Psalm 90 that each of our lives in this transitional home has an end point – one that calls us to apply the wisdom gained from that perspective to every area of our lives: 'The length of our days is seventy years – or eighty, if we have the strength; yet their span is but trouble and sorrow, for they quickly pass, and we fly away.... Teach us to number our days aright, that we may gain a heart of wisdom' (vv. 10, 12). A final day of accounting is coming, it cannot be postponed, and 'nothing in all creation is hidden from God's sight.... the eyes of him to whom we must give account' (Heb. 4:13).

What's the point of all this? Simply this: *few things, like death, will put life in perspective.* And few things, like accountability, will put obedience in perspective. This life is transitional; it can prepare us to be welcomed into our new, eternal home. And it provides us with a lifetime of opportunities to invite others along, beginning with our own families. In the process, it will call us to a constant preoccupation with eternity, and the One who fills it and qualifies us for it.

In the following chapters, I'd like to show you a picture of a godly home, based on the practice of our Puritan predecessors in the faith. I wish I could simply show you a picture of my own family and home as an example. But the reminder of our many shortcomings, and outright failures, makes us more of a distortion of that picture than a model. Yet we're learning, and are growing toward that end. What lies at the center of this maturing process is an ever-growing understanding that our lives, individually and collectively as a family, must be centered around Christ. Not just around his finished work on the cross, but also around his ongoing work in our lives through his Holy Spirit as he prepares to welcome us to our new home in heaven. This is the perspective that I believe most powerfully impacts upon building and enjoying a godly home, all as a way of attractively displaying and persuasively commending the glory of God in the life of a Christian family.

Now we see but a poor reflection as in a mirror; then we shall see face to face. Now I know in part; then I shall know fully, even as I am fully known (1 Cor. 13:12).

1

PREPARING TO DIE WELL
ECCLESIASTES 7:1-14

A good name is better than fine perfume,
and the day of death better than the day of birth.
It is better to go to a house of mourning
than to go to a house of feasting,
for death is the destiny of every man;
the living should take this to heart.
Sorrow is better than laughter,
because a sad face is good for the heart.
The heart of the wise is in the house of mourning,
but the heart of fools is in the house of pleasure.
It is better to heed a wise man's rebuke
than to listen to the song of fools.
Like the crackling of thorns under the pot,
so is the laughter of fools.
This too is meaningless.
Extortion turns a wise man into a fool,
and a bribe corrupts the heart.
The end of a matter is better than its beginning,
and patience is better than pride.
Do not be quickly provoked in your spirit,
for anger resides in the lap of fools.
Do not say, 'Why were the old days better than these?'
For it is not wise to ask such questions.
Wisdom, like an inheritance, is a good thing
and benefits those who see the sun.
Wisdom is a shelter as money is a shelter,
but the advantage of knowledge is this:

that wisdom preserves the life of its possessor.
Consider what God has done:
Who can straighten what he has made crooked?
When times are good, be happy;
but when times are bad, consider:
God has made the one as well as the other.
Therefore, a man cannot discover anything about his future.

Not long ago, I was paging though a catalog that listed a number of newly published books and my attention was drawn to one in particular that had a truly intriguing title: Erwin Lutzer's book, *One Minute After You Die*. A captivating title for anyone with an interest in what lies beyond the point of death. It goes right to the heart of a question I was asked not long ago by an eighty-five year old member of the church I pastor: 'When I close my eyes in death, and exhale my last breath, and in that instant, when I open my eyes on the other side and inhale my first breath there – what will that be like? What will I see? What will I hear? What will I smell? Will there be other, new, senses that I've never before experienced? What will it be like?'

Solomon, the writer of the passage we're considering, addresses that question in a stunning manner. He tells us in the first verse that 'the day of one's death is *better* than the day of one's birth'. These words fly in the face of nearly every part of conventional wisdom, yet at the same time, they present us with a renewed sense of spiritual vision and perspective, largely because they take the long view. This verse looks at eternity with unhindered eyes: 'the day of one's death is *better* than the day of one's birth.'

Now, I don't know about you, but when I read that verse, my first thought is to ask, 'How can that possibly be?' I've personally been present at the birth of each of my four children, and I can assure you, there could not possibly be a better day than each of those four birth-days! I've also been present at the death of the woman who gave birth to these children, a woman I loved more than life itself. I held her in my arms as she breathed her last breaths and felt her heart stop its beating after only thirty-two years of life. If you and I were to look at the day of birth and the day of death from the perspective of the uncontainable joy, or the inescapable sorrow, that it brings to the family and loved ones of the one who has just been born or has just died, how can we possibly agree with King Solomon, the writer of these words, that the day of one's death is *better* than the day of one's birth? That's the immediate question that needs to be answered as we seek a renewed sense of spiritual vision and perspective.

Yet in order to answer that question, there is an even deeper question that needs to be addressed. For whom are King Solomon's words true? About whom can it be said that the day of one's death is better than the day of one's birth? Clearly, not everyone's day of death will be better than their day of birth. The Lord Jesus himself addresses that subject in Matthew 26, when he talks about Judas, the one who was about to betray him, and he uses the same word, 'better', to compare Judas' day of birth to the day of his death, only the comparison is set in a somewhat different context. Jesus says, 'Woe to the man who will betray me, for it would be *better* for him, had he never been born.' There is an apparent contradiction here, isn't there? 'The day of one's death is better than the day of one's birth – It would be better for him to never have been born.' So we need to unpack this, and look very carefully at what Scripture teaches about those two questions. How can it possibly be true that the day of one's death is better than the day of one's birth? For whom is this true?

In answer to the first question, it is clear that Solomon has stepped back and is taking the long view. He's looking at life and death from the perspective of eternity. He is looking at the result and effect of the day of one's birth in comparison to the result and effect of the day of one's death. William Perkins, in the introduction to his treatise, *The Right Manner of Dying Well*, reflects on this verse and writes: 'The day of one's birth is an entrance into all misery. Whereas the day of one's death, when joined with God and reformed life, is an entrance into a greater degree of eternal life.' The birth of a child is truly an awesome and absolutely overwhelming event and day. Yet even Moses, in Psalm 90:10, tells us that at best, our lives are comprised of trouble and sorrow, 'The length of our days is 70 years – or 80, if we have the strength; yet their span is but trouble and sorrow, for they quickly pass, and we fly away.' The day of birth initiates this life, a life that may reach to 70, 80, 90, or even 100 years, but Moses says what Solomon affirms, 'The span is but trouble and sorrow, and they quickly pass and we fly away.'

Job refers to the same thing in 5:7, of the book that bears his name, when he writes, 'As surely as sparks fly upward, man is born unto trouble.' It is these repeated affirmations that lead Solomon to write in verse 2, 'It is better to go to a house of mourning than to a house of feasting for death is the destiny of every man; the living must take this to heart.' Death is inevitable, unavoidable. The day of my death and yours is approaching, and will arrive, unless the Lord Jesus should return first. Solomon recognizes that though this life offers us some very rich and rewarding experiences, there is something so much greater for which we were created that this life never even begins to approach. At the same time, he also recognizes that there is no doorway to that experience apart from death. *The living must take this to heart.*[1] This isn't just Old Testament thinking. The apostle Paul affirms the same truth in Philippians 1:21: 'For me to live is Christ, and to die is gain. Therefore I desire to depart and be with Christ, which is *better by far.*'

. William Perkins centers his entire argument on one fundamental answer: Solomon is teaching us that only those who are *rightly prepared* for the inevitability of death will find that the day of their death will be better than the day of their birth. This he unpacks and develops by showing us four primary duties that are absolutely necessary in preparing to die well – duties that not only must be understood, but also must be embraced, and wholeheartedly pursued, in order for the day of one's death to be better than the day of one's birth.

The first duty is *to learn to meditate on death in the time of life.* Again this flies in the face of most everything that is normal and customary in our culture, because we relentlessly ignore death, joke about death, and by our attitudes and actions deny the inevitability of death. Our culture has so neatly sanitized the subject of death and carefully distanced itself from it, that the idea of deliberately *meditating* on death during the time of life is all but absurd to our contemporary thought process.

In Luke 12:16-20, Jesus speaks as clearly to our culture as he did to the one in which he lived when he told this parable:

---

[1] Perkins, William, *A Salve for a Sicke Man, or The Right Manner of Dying Well* (London: University of Cambridge, Microfilm, 1616). It should be noted that not all commentators agree with Perkins' interpretation of this passage. Some believe this passage presents the reflection of the skeptic who sees all of life from the perspective of futility.

The ground of a certain rich man produced a good crop. He thought to himself, 'What shall I do? I have no place to store my crops.' Then he said, 'This is what I'll do. I will tear down my barns and build bigger ones, and there I will store all my grain and my goods. And I'll say to myself, 'You have plenty of good things laid up for many years. Take life easy; eat, drink and be merry.' But God said to him, 'You fool! This very night your life will be demanded from you. Then who will get what you have prepared for yourself?'

Why worry about death? Why allow our minds to think in such a negative and depressing direction? Even the Christian finds it much easier to say, 'Why meditate on death when I've got so much to be grateful for, and I can set my thoughts, affections, and pursuits on these things? Let's just be happy and grateful for what God has given us, and let's not worry about death!' This is an especially great temptation for those who are young. Our youth have a tendency to think about their lives and future as if they are invincible and indestructible, and then are shocked when one of their own is killed in a car accident, or is diagnosed with a debilitating, or even fatal, illness. In Isaiah 28:15, the prophet addresses that pattern of thinking: 'You boast that we have entered into a covenant with death, with the grave we have made an agreement. When an overwhelming scourge sweeps by, it cannot touch us, for we have made a lie our refuge and falsehood has become our hiding place.'

The prophet is warning against the assumption that only 'someone else' will be diagnosed with cancer, or Muscular Sclerosis, or AIDS; only a stranger can have the sudden car accident or the injury that may cost a life. 'These things only happen to people I don't know, but I'm invincible, I'm immune – it won't happen to me. It won't, it can't, touch me.'

Yet reality has an unassuming way of asserting its inescapable presence. Go to the cemetery and look at the dates on the gravestones. Every time I drive through the cemetery where the body of my first wife is buried, my attention is drawn to a small granite stone cut in the shape of a 'Smurf' cartoon character, engraved with a child's name and a date of birth and date of death just a few years apart. I don't suspect his parents anticipated commissioning that gravestone the day they drove to the hospital with his mother in labor. An unexpected death, and for his parents, a terribly painful death. None of us expects our death to be as sudden or as soon as it may be. We always assume we have so much more time. Psalm 39:4 says, 'Show me, O LORD, my life's end and the number of my days; let me know how fleeting is my life.' Moses prays in Psalm 90:12, 'Teach us to number our days aright, that we may gain a heart of wisdom.' The first duty in preparing to die well is to meditate on death during the time of life.

The second duty is *to make absolutely certain that eternal life is yours* – that you are a possessor of an eternal inheritance in God's presence. But what establishes that certainty? A feeling? A conviction? Or is it something much more tangible and measurable?

Imagine being in a classroom with thirty other students and the teacher looks directly at you and says, 'You are an exemplary student, and you've done excellent work in your studies.' What would lead a teacher to make that kind of statement? Is it simply a result of being in class when you are scheduled to be there, taking meticulous notes, and faithfully studying them? Is that all that is necessary? I wish that were true. I would have avoided a great deal of anxiety during my years in school had that been the case! The anxiety comes when the exam arrives. It is only the *results* of the examination that enable us to see the degree to which we truly possess the knowledge to which we've been exposed. Often times you come away from an exam thinking, 'I did well!', and then the teacher returns the graded exam and reality sets in. How well I remember!

The apostle Paul employs this imagery in 2 Corinthians 13:5: 'Examine yourselves to see whether you are in the faith: test yourselves. Do you not realize that Christ Jesus is in you – unless, of course, you fail the test?' Paul is reflecting the certainty that there is a final exam coming. On the day we stand before God's throne and the Book of Life is open, there will be a one-question exam: 'Is your name written there?' (Rev. 20:15; 21:27). If your name is there, you will be ushered into his eternal presence. If it is not there, you will be ushered into eternal damnation. But Paul's primary concern in this verse is to remind us that there is not just a final exam to be anticipated, but also the preliminary exams that make up every day of our lives as we prepare for the final exam. Paul simply tells us to schedule our own exams and test ourselves. William Perkins identifies for us the three exam questions that each of us needs to address to our daily experience.

Question one: Do I possess a saving knowledge of Jesus Christ? Contemporarily, we could ask the diagnostic questions of the Evangelism Explosion Gospel Presentation: 'If I were to die tonight, do I know for certain where I would spend eternity? If I found myself standing before God's throne and he asked me, "Why should I let you into my kingdom?" how accurately and convincingly would I be able to answer that question? Am I able to pull out a piece of paper right now and, without hesitation, answer these questions?' The answer 'yes' would have to be followed by several affirmations:

first: I know I am a sinner and justly deserve eternal punishment (Rom. 3:23; 6:23);

second: I know that Christ died on the cross, in my place, as my substitute in punishment, and that God placed my sin on Christ and unleashed the unabated fury of his wrath against my sin on Christ (Isa. 53:4-5);

third: that Christ, in exchange for my sin, has freely credited to me the riches of his perfect righteousness (Rom. 4:6, 24) and has fully clothed me in his perfect righteousness (Isa. 61:10) so that when God looks at me, he will say, 'I have declared you to be perfectly righteous and you meet my requirement to be holy even as I am holy' (2 Cor. 5:21; 1 Pet. 1:16; Heb. 12:14).

1 Peter 3:15 says, 'Always be prepared to give an answer to everyone who asks you to give the reason for the hope that you have.' How well would you score on that first exam question?

Question two: Do I have a peace of conscience through repentance, forgiveness and reconciliation? Not just do I have a saving knowledge of Christ, but the peace of conscience that is the outgrowth of that saving knowledge of Christ. Paul says in Romans 14:17: 'For the kingdom of God is not a matter of eating and drinking, but of righteousness, peace (of conscience) and joy in the Holy Spirit.' It's interesting that the command to be prepared to give an answer for the eternal hope that we have expressed in 1 Peter 3:15 is followed with 'keeping a clear conscience' (v. 16).

Question three: Do I have a will that is humbly submitted to the authority of God's Word? The question looks not only to whether it is my conscious determination to maintain a will submitted to the authority of God's Word, but does my life display the effect of a will so submitted? Is it evident to my family members, co-workers, neighbors, and fellow church members? These are the exam questions that you need to be asking yourself – questions to which you must respond conclusively and convincingly. 'Examine yourselves,' as Paul says, 'to see whether you are in the faith. Test yourselves. Do you not realize that Jesus Christ is in you? Unless, of course, you failed the test?'

So, the first two duties necessary in preparing for a day of death that will be better than the day of your birth are: (1) Meditate on death during the time of life; and (2) Make certain that you truly possess eternal life.

The third duty is *to deal radically with sin – both past and present sin*. Deal radically with it, for there is nothing casual or neutral about any of our sin. Perkins illustrates this by using the imagery of a man doing battle with a mighty dragon. He has one of two alternatives: he must kill or be killed. He cannot peacefully co-exist with his mortal enemy. The application is plain. An individual made righteous through the shed blood of Christ applied to his life cannot peacefully co-exist with sin in his life. We cannot say, 'I know this is wrong, but it's not that bad; it's not going to lead me astray. I can handle this.' When the Spirit of God identifies your sin as he shines the light of his Word through the lens of your conscience and says, 'You know and I know that this is wrong,' then you are faced with a choice. You must either kill that sin, by God's grace, or you will be killed by it. The present tense is an even better way of describing these two alternatives: By God's grace, you must be killing the sin in your life or it will be killing you. You cannot peacefully co-exist with sin in your life. Paul in Romans 8:13 says, 'If you live according to the sinful nature, you will die; but if by the Spirit, you put to death the misdeeds of the body, you will live.' Again, in Colossians 3:5 he says, 'Put to death, therefore, whatever belongs to the sinful nature.' Kill or be killed when it comes to sin in your life.

The final duty in preparing to die well is that if we are to die well in the end, *we must learn to die daily while we are living*. Paul writes of this in 1 Corinthians 15:31: 'I die every day – I mean that, brothers – just as surely as I glory over you in Christ Jesus our Lord.' We find this also in 1 Peter 2:24: 'Christ bore our sins in his body so that we might die to sins and live for righteousness.' Both apostles are referring to a daily dying to self, a putting to death the sinful desires that war against the new desires that God has placed within us by his Spirit. A dying to our constant insistence upon our own rights. A dying to our unwillingness to suffer for the gospel. A dying to our unwillingness to be inconvenienced or made to feel uncomfortable because of the demands of the cross. If we are to be prepared to die well in the end we must be dying daily as we live. Jesus said: 'If anyone would come after me, he must deny himself, take up his cross daily, and follow.'(Matt. 16:24) That's dying to self.

Memento mori is the Latin phrase that is used to represent a common theme in English literature. It means *remember that you must die.* Some might take this as a morbid theme, especially those who believe that we should be entirely preoccupied with life and all that it offers. But it is the ongoing reminder of this theme throughout all of life that forces us to deal rightly with the four duties William Perkins prescribes in preparing for our eternal home.

When your earthly life draws to a close, the way you now respond to these four duties will determine which of these two statements will then be true of you: 'The day of his death was better than the day of his birth' or 'It would have been better for him to have never been born.' One of those two statements must be proclaimed of the life of every one who has ever lived. But only one will be true of your life, for there is no middle ground.

The story is told of vice-president Calvin Coolidge who, during the 1920s, was presiding over the senate, when during a heated debate, one senator angrily snapped at another senator, 'Go to hell.' The offended senator was flabbergasted! His mouth dropped open and after a few moments of stunned silence, turned his attention to Coolidge and insisted he address the impropriety of those words. Coolidge had been absent-mindedly flipping through the pages of a book, and he casually looked up and said, 'I have been consulting the Rules Manual, and you don't have to go.' What was intended to be an off-handed understatement, points us to a sobering reality: there is a 'rules manual' in which God reveals to us his determined will, and in it he says that unless you stand forgiven by the blood of Christ and are clothed in his righteousness, you are convicted and condemned already and *must* go to hell. That's what the rules manual of Scripture affirms. Jesus says in John 3:18, 'That person who rejects the gospel stands condemned already because he has not believed in the name of God's one and only Son.' Apart from Christ, we are convicted and condemned already, and are simply waiting for the eternal sentence to be executed. It's just a matter of time.

Over the past several decades it has become increasingly popular to believe that the duration of time a person condemned to hell must remain there is limited. The assumption is that God could not possibly punish *eternally* without at some point saying, 'OK, you have been there long enough. It serves me no reasonable purpose to continue your torment forever, so I'll just end your miserable existence – you are annihilated.' That person then ceases to exist, in any form, even in the memories of others who knew him or her. It is as if that person never existed. The assumption is that a good God, a just God, a merciful God, will punish *sufficiently* but he won't punish *eternally*.

The problem with that rationale is that Scripture uses the same language to talk about the duration of the experience of the one in heaven as it does to talk about the duration of the experience of the one in hell. Identical language. Revelation 20:10, for example, says, 'They and the devil who deceived them were thrown into the lake of burning sulfur and there they will be tormented day and night for ever and ever.' Revelation 22:5 follows with, 'There will be no more night. They will not need the light of a lamp or the light of the sun, for the Lord God will give them light. And they will reign for ever and ever.' Identical language is used to describe the duration of the experience of the one in God's presence in heaven where there will be rejoicing in the presence of the Lamb and all his angels for ever and ever; and the duration of the experience of those in hell, where there will be weeping and gnashing of teeth forever and ever. The day of your death will be better than the day of your birth, *or* it would have been better for you had you never been born.

Preparing to die well ultimately centers on one fundamental issue, which may be illustrated with two verses of Scripture. The first is Revelation 14:10 where John warns that 'the wicked will drink the wine of God's fury which has been poured full-strength into the cup of his wrath.' Hold in your mind, for just a moment, the imagery of the cup of God's wrath, from which the wicked will drink the wine of his fury. Then turn the attention of your mind's eye to the garden of Gethsemane, recorded in Matthew 26, where three times Jesus pleads with his Father, 'Father, if it is possible, let this cup pass from Me.'

What was this cup that Jesus pleaded with his Father to remove? It's the same cup that the apostle John refers to in Revelation 14. It is the cup that the unrepentant sinner will drink for all eternity in hell. One of two things is true about you today and will be true for all eternity as a result. Either you will trust the Son of God to have drunk that cup on your behalf, or you will drink it yourself for all eternity in hell. This, ultimately, is what lies at the heart of preparing to die well.

On August 25, 1996, a cloudless Sunday morning, as churches all over our country were celebrating worship, the earthly life of my beautiful young wife was quietly drawing to a close. I held her gently in my arms as she labored for her final breaths. I was able to see with my own eyes an incredible woman passing from this life into life eternal. I believe with unshakable certainty that when Amy went from my arms into the arms of her heavenly husband, the Lord Jesus Christ, the first words she heard as he embraced her were, 'Well done! Well done, good and faithful servant.'

Amy didn't hear those words because she was a good woman. She was that, and so much more! But Amy heard those words because she had embraced for herself the life-transforming reality of the cross. She had learned to meditate on the inevitability of death, and had made certain that she possessed eternal life. She knew that at the cross, the infinite, eternal, and unchangeable God had unleashed the full fury of his wrath against her sin, which he had placed upon his Son. His Son died a brutal death, so that she could come to her own death without fear. Amy had embraced these truths to be her very own, and there was no part of her life that was not impacted by the reality of that cross. She displayed a heart determined to deal radically with her sin – a heart willing to die daily while she was living. All of that enabled her to come to the end of her life with a sense of purpose and with a joyful sense of anticipation.

The last lucid conversation I had with her was at the hospital, in the middle of the night about three weeks before she died.

I asked her, 'Sweetheart, do you know what's happening to you?' She nodded her head slowly, but deliberately, and said, 'I'm going home.' I asked her how she felt about that. With a quiet calm, she simply said, 'I'm okay, I know whom I'm going to see,' and drifted off to sleep.

There is a real sense of delight in knowing that Amy, along with Paul, could say, 'For me to live is Christ, to die is gain.' This is not some plastic thing we say at funerals, but don't really believe. This is our ultimate reality, and this is our eternal hope. That's what gives meaning and purpose to the life that you and I still live today.

I don't know where you stand, nor am I the one who searches hearts. I find that it is easy to maintain a very good front and to make it appear that everything in life is rolling along smoothly. But take a moment to step back from those things that preoccupy your immediate attention and look at the eternity ahead. From this perspective you discover that God has prepared a future for you that makes the very best of this life seem comparatively insignificant. There is an eternal home which God has prepared for his children, and to which he is even now drawing them. Yet at the same time, there is also an eternal hell to be avoided. You may be wrestling with these things because you've never embraced for yourself the offer that Christ has made through the gospel. You've never exchanged your sin for his perfect righteousness. You stand at a crossroads of decision and must choose, for though none of us knows the day of our death, we affirm with King Solomon, 'It is better to go to the house of mourning than to go to the house of feasting, for death is the destiny of every man. *The living must take this to heart.*' I urge you to choose carefully, knowing that in so doing, you are preparing to die well, even today.

QUESTIONS FOR FURTHER STUDY AND REFLECTION

1. What are you most looking forward to and working toward, and what eternal value is there in it? (Phil. 1:21; Gal. 2:20)

2. To what extent is the inevitability of your own death part of your daily perspective? Are you living as if death is only an illusion and will not touch your life? (Ps. 39:4; 90:12)

3. Are you certain that you possess eternal life?

Note: The issue is not simply, 'Do you believe you are going to heaven?' Many are inclined to answer that question in the affirmative, without any Biblical basis for their answer. Rather, the issue is, 'How have you responded to the authority of Scripture in its condemnation of our sin, its offer of redeeming grace, and its requirement that we embrace for ourselves the forgiveness and righteousness of Christ?' (2 Cor. 13:5)

4. To whom have the individual members of your family declared their eternal allegiance, and on what basis do you believe this to be true? (Matt. 10:32-33)

5. Are you keeping short accounts with sin in your life? Or are you rationalizing and minimizing those things in your life that God's Word clearly identifies as sin? (Rom. 8:13; Col. 3:5)

6. Of what sins have you repented before God this last week? Whose forgiveness have you sought this last week? Is the example of your life teaching the members of your family the importance of repentance and forgiveness? (1 John 1:9)

7. Is the death of Christ on your behalf leading you to progressively die to sin and live for righteousness? (1 Cor. 15:31; 1 Pet. 2:24)

8. Which motive most often influences your desires and choices: the pursuit of your own comfort and convenience, or your submission to the daily demands of the cross of Christ? (Matt. 10:38)

2

THE PRIVILEGE OF SUBMITTING
TO ONE ANOTHER
EPHESIANS 5:15–33

'If we are to die well in the end,' William Perkins wrote, 'we must learn to die daily while we are living.' While this most certainly includes a dying to self and a dying to the sinful desires that war against the desires that God has placed within us by his Spirit, I find that the most difficult part of our experience to which we must die is our insistence upon what we perceive as being our rights. This is why Jesus said in Luke 9:23: 'If anyone would come after me, *he must deny himself*, take up his cross daily, and follow me.' There is an almost imperceptible line between right and privilege, but the pursuit of each manifests itself in profoundly different ways. Rights are insisted upon and demanded, while privileges are celebrated and received with humble gratitude.

Taking this one step further, the roles which we are called to fulfill in the context of the godly family can be viewed either as an extension of our rights to be demanded, or as an extension of our privilege to be celebrated. The way we perceive our God-ordained roles will determine the manner in which we relate to our spouse and to the rest of those in our family. With that in mind, we may affirm again that few things more attractively display and persuasively commend the glory of God in the life of a Christian than a Christ-centered marriage and the Christ-centered family relationships that grow out of that marriage. So how do we rightly perceive our individual role, and collective roles, as members of a Christ-centered family? One husband, for example, said, 'In our house, I decide the big things, like what to do about welfare or healthcare reform, whether or not NAFTA helped our trade status, whether the President should change his posture toward foreign policy, and those sorts of things. My wife decides the smaller things, like what house we're going to live in, what car we're going to buy, what college my kids will attend, and those sorts of things.' While by comparison, foreign policy seems more significant than domestic living arrangements, this man's definition of role is manipulated to justify the abdication of his God-given role.

John Chrysostom, Patriarch of Constantinople in the fifth century, wrote, 'If they (the husband and wife) perform their proper duties, everything around them acquires firmness and stability.'[1] So how should we properly perceive our roles as members of a Christ-centered family?

The apostle Paul presents us with a broad answer to that question throughout his letters as he repeatedly affirms, 'Role is an outgrowth of identity.' Who we are determines what we do. If we then rightly understand who we are in Christ, then the question of role (and the tension between right and privilege) becomes a much more straightforward issue to address. Let's consider what Scripture teaches us regarding our identity, and the roles that flow from it.

In the last three chapters of his letter to the Ephesians, Paul talks about life in the covenant community. Between verses 20 and 22 of the fifth chapter, we find a significant transitional statement. He ends verse 20 with a collective command, addressed to all in the church: 'always giving thanks to God the Father for everything, in the name of our Lord Jesus Christ.' In verse 22, he begins a series of commands directed at individual categories of people in the church, beginning specifically with wives: 'Wives, submit to your husbands as to the Lord.' But the transitional statement, which I believe is addressed to all in the church of Jesus Christ, is verse 21: 'Submit to one another out of reverence for Christ.' This has been defined, by some, as 'mutual submission' or a recognition that each of us is accountable to submit to one another, within the context of our roles, as an expression of our submission to Christ. All of this recognizes that as created beings, our identity is wrapped up in the

---

[1] *Puritan Sermons, 1659–1689*, Vol.2 (1674. Reprint, Wheaton, Ill: Richard Owen Roberts Publishers, 1981), p. 303.

fact that we have been designed to line up under, and submit to, the authority of Christ, the creator and redeemer of the church.

This concept of submission is found over thirty times in the New Testament alone, again and again reminding us that the whole mentality of the Christian life as we relate to one another is to be one of humility and submissiveness. Whether it's in the context of the church or the Christian family, arrogance and self-serving pride hold no place in our identity in Christ.

I must very quickly add that none of this is possible for us in the context of our human nature, which is why Paul says in Ephesians 5:18: 'Do not get drunk on wine, which leads to debauchery. Instead, *be filled with the Spirit.*' This is the only means by which we will ever know the capacity to give expression to our identity in Christ in a way that expresses humility and submissiveness, and in so doing, display and commend the glory of Christ. The fulfilling of our roles within the Christ-centered family demands nothing short of the ongoing filling of the Holy Spirit.

The Puritans generally saw this filling as impacting directly upon one primary area of our experience: the conscience. From their perspective, the conscience is an inexpressible and divine lens within us which constantly evaluates our choices, affections, and motives while recalling our responsibilities or duty to mind. The conscience is the lens through which the Holy Spirit shines the light of God's Word upon our experience. They taught that we respond to this activity of the Holy Spirit through a process they called 'casuistry', or cases of conscience. God's Word was to be held up against the details of our practice, words, and affections in a way that would move us forward in a manner neither robbed of joy, nor settled in complacency. They often referred to Paul's words in 2 Corinthians 1:12: 'Now this is our boast: *Our conscience testifies* that we have conducted ourselves in the world, and especially in relations with you, in the holiness and sincerity that are from God. We have done so not according to worldly wisdom, but according to God's grace.'

Yet in our fallen state, the conscience functions accurately only to the extent that it is informed and constrained by the Word of God. This, in their view, is how arrogance and self-serving pride are progressively rejected, and how humility and a spirit of Christ-centered submission is deliberately fostered.

Before examining the distinct character of the roles of the husband and wife (male and female), we need to examine what the Puritans saw as being the mutually held aspects of the identity of both husband and wife.

First, there was the unique dignity with which both were equally created. In Genesis 1:26-27, God says, 'Let us make *man* in our image, in our likeness, and let *them* rule over the fish of the sea and the birds of the air, over the livestock, over all the earth, and over all the creatures that move along the ground. So God created *man* in his own image, in the image of God he created *him*; *male and female he* created *them.*' While both reflect the dignity of being created in the image of God, neither fully reflects that image without the completion of the other. Both find the authority and mandate to rule over the rest of God's created order wrapped up in their identity as the only beings in this universe expressly created in the image of God.

Second, the identity of both the man and the woman reflects, to the same total extent and radical degree, the utter depravity of a sinful nature. Women, in terms of their nature, are not more sinful than men, nor is the nature of men more sinful than that of women. Paul says in Romans 3:10-19:

> As it is written: 'There is no one righteous, not even one; there is no one who understands, no one who seeks God. All have turned away, they have together become worthless; there is no one who does good, not even one. Their throats are open graves; their tongues practice deceit. The poison of vipers is on their lips. Their mouths are full of cursing and bitterness. Their feet are swift to shed blood; ruin and misery mark their ways, and the way of peace they do not know. There is no fear of God before their eyes.' Now we know that whatever the law says, it says to those who are under the law, so that every mouth may be silenced and the whole world held accountable to God.

In Ephesians 2:1-3 Paul says:

> As for you, you were dead in your transgressions and sins, in which you used to live when you followed the ways of this world and of the ruler of the kingdom of the air, the spirit who is now at work in those who are disobedient. *All of us* also lived among them at one time, gratifying the cravings of our sinful nature and

following its desires and thoughts. Like the rest, we were by nature objects of wrath.

Although both the man and the woman began equally with the dignity of being created in the image of God, as a result of the fall the identity of both man and woman now reflect, to the same total extent and radical degree, the utter depravity of a sinful nature.

Third, the identity of both the man and the woman reflects an equal access to God's redeeming grace. In other words, neither the man nor the woman is more redeemable than the other. In Christ, there is absolute equality in terms of forgiveness, redemption, and reconciliation. A man's union with Christ is no different from a woman's. The acceptance in Christ that both a man and a woman may share, and the sense of belonging they then treasure, is an area of absolute equality in their identity. Paul writes in Galatians 3:27-28: 'For all of you who were baptized into Christ have clothed yourselves with Christ. There is neither Jew nor Greek, slave nor free, *male nor female*, for you are all one in Christ Jesus.'

It has been noted that wherever the gospel of Jesus Christ has been proclaimed, and consequently embraced, the role of women has been elevated to unprecedented levels. That's simply because the gospel clearly teaches the redemption of women as equal to the redemption of men. The redeemed identity of a woman, and the role that grows out of that identity, is then not only elevated, but radically transformed – just as a man's identity and role are. Because of these underlying assumptions, the Puritan Richard Steele wrote, 'Let the sex (gender) of each of you by degrees cease to be discerned, and both of you begin to make serious preparation for that heavenly life in which there is no distinction of the sexes.'[2]

It is in this light that the difference between right and privilege becomes even more evident, and the pursuit of each manifests itself in an even more radical manner. What rights can be insisted upon when we perceive our redemption, as men and women, husbands and wives, from the perspective of who we are in Christ? All that we are and all that we have in union with Christ is nothing short of the highest privilege imaginable, and is therefore to be treasured, celebrated, and received with humble gratitude. This is what lies

---

[2] Ibid., p. 279.

at the foundation of our understanding of the unique character of the roles of the husband and wife to which we have been called by Christ.

From this perspective, the husband and wife have a mutual responsibility to deliberately unite with one another, or as the King James Version translates it, to 'cleave' to one another. A responsibility that recognizes what the Lord said in Genesis 2:18: 'It is not good for the man to be *alone*. I will make a helper suitable for him.' The aloneness was to be abated and overcome through uniting or cleaving. But it is not the husband alone who is to cleave. Both are charged to cleave to one another. This is seen in Genesis 2:24: 'For this reason a man will leave his father and mother and be united to his wife, *and they will become one flesh.*

This 'one flesh' principle is what lies at the heart of most, if not all, Biblical teaching on marriage, pointing to the unreserved commitment to the perfect intimacy God designed for a married couple, an intimacy that reflects the beauty of the relationship between Christ and the church. It is symbolized in a marriage by the sexual union between a husband and wife, but is certainly not limited to that. 'One flesh' reflects the intimacy that is to be celebrated, embraced, and enjoyed in all their life together. It is in this context that Genesis 1:27-28 addresses the man and the woman, the crowning masterpiece of God's creative work, and says, 'So God created man in his own image, in the image of God he created him; male and female he created them. God blessed *them* and said to *them,* "Be fruitful and increase in number; fill the earth and subdue it."'

Now we must shift our focus slightly. Because there is absolute equality in our identity in Christ before God, there is, by necessity, a degree of equality in role – though all the while understanding that there is yet significant difference between the role of the husband and the role of the wife. Let's consider, for a moment, the places in the role of the husband and the role of the wife where there is equality. For where there is equality in role, there is also equality in responsibility. Again, Richard Steele said, 'It is not in the *having* of a husband or wife that brings contentment, but in the *mutual discharge* of both their duties, and *this* is what makes their lives... a heaven upon earth.'[3]

---

[3] Ibid., p. 274.

So what are those duties which must, by virtue of the equality of the husband's and wife's identity, be mutually discharged?

First, there is *a mutual obligation to love one another*. We may begin by citing the eleven times this command is repeated in the New Testament.

'A new command I give you: Love one another. As I have loved you, so you must love one another' (John 13:34);

'By this all men will know that you are my disciples, if you love one another' (John 13:35);

'Let no debt remain outstanding, except the continuing debt to love one another, for he who loves his fellow man (and wife/ husband) has fulfilled the law' (Rom. 13:8);

'Now that you have purified yourselves by obeying the truth so that you have sincere love for your brothers, love one another deeply, from the heart' (1 Pet. 1:22);

'This is the message you heard from the beginning: We should love one another' (1 John 3:11);

'And this is his command: to believe in the name of his Son, Jesus Christ, and to love one another as he commanded us' (1 John 3:23);

'Dear friends, let us love one another, for love comes from God. Everyone who loves has been born of God and knows God' (1 John 4:7);

'Dear friends, since God so loved us, we also ought to love one another' (1 John 4:11);

'No one has ever seen God; but if we love one another, God lives in us and his love is made complete in us' (1 John 4:12);

'And now, dear lady, I am not writing you a new command but one we have had from the beginning. I ask that we love one another' (2 John 1:5).

Broadly speaking, all Christians share the responsibility to love one another, a responsibility that is to be mutually discharged regardless of gender.

But some would be quick to say that Scripture generally places the responsibility of taking the initiative to love on the husband's shoulders. After all, Paul tells the husbands in the church at Ephesus, 'Husbands, love your wives, just as Christ loved the church and gave himself up for her' (Eph. 5:25). In Ephesians 5:28, he says, 'In this same way, husbands ought to love their wives as their own bodies. He who loves his wife loves himself.' Again, in Colossians 3:19, he says, 'Husbands, love your wives and do not be harsh with them.' But in Titus 2:4-5, he gives a specific command relative to the woman's responsibility to take the initiative in loving her husband: 'train the younger women to love their husbands and children, to be self-controlled and pure, to be busy at home, to be kind, and to be subject to their husbands, so that no one will malign the word of God.' Self-control, purity, busyness, kindness, and subjection to their husbands are all important virtues for a wife, but first and foremost, Paul says, 'train the younger women to love their husbands', even before he commands that they be taught to love their children!

Richard Steele tells the story of a wealthy Englishwoman, Clara Cerventa, who lived more than three centuries ago. Her husband, Valdaura, became ill, and finally was bedridden. He developed sores no one else was willing to clean and dress. She cared for him, provided for him, loved him, and nurtured him for ten years. In the process, she was forced to sell all her property, even her jewelry, in order to support her husband and family. Finally Valdaura died. Her friends came to her home, more to congratulate her in finally being free of this burden than to console her. Her response? 'I would be willing to purchase my dear Valdaura again with the loss of all my five children.'[4]

By virtue of the equality of the husband's and wife's identity, the first duty which must be mutually discharged is to love one another.

The second duty is *to maintain faithfulness to one another*. In 1 Corinthians 7:2, Paul writes: 'Let every man have his own wife, and every woman have her own husband.' There is a certain exclusivity to this command, marked out more by understatement than by deliberate emphasis. It goes beyond simply leaving one's father

[4] Ibid., p. 292.

and mother and cleaving to one's wife or husband. It points to the permanence of unswerving fidelity to the one with whom you have exchanged vows.

I used to think that infidelity was primarily a male problem, having seen more men than I care to remember leave their families for other women. I was convinced that as I preached on this subject, it was primarily into the eyes of the men in my congregation that I needed to be looking – until the last several years. I have listened to the painful accounts and have watched with horror how one wife after another has left her husband (and children) for another person. As recently as this past month, I was distressed to learn of the grief that had come to the home of one of my brothers in Christ. He was faced with the tremendously difficult task of informing his children that his wife and their mother had left them to pursue her dreams with a man she had met through a chat room on the internet.

In conversations with men and women whose marriages had been touched (again: understatement) by infidelity, I've concluded that one of the first steps toward marital infidelity is revealing to others what should be kept secret about one's spouse. Conversely, if you wish to safeguard your marriage from infidelity, then begin by remaining faithful to one another's secrets. Violating the integrity of your marriage vows is much easier once you've violated the integrity of your wife's or husband's secrets. If your marriage is to remain sacred, then so must your secrets.

The third duty which, by virtue of the equality of the husband's and wife's identity, must be mutually discharged, is *to exercise patience with, and toward, one another.* Paul frames the fourth chapter of his letter to the church at Ephesus with nearly identical bookends at both ends of the chapter. In verses 1-2 he says: 'As a prisoner for the Lord, then, I urge you to live a life worthy of the calling you have received. Be completely humble and gentle; be patient, bearing with one another in love.' At the end of that chapter, he reiterates his challenge toward patient, forgiving, forbearance (v. 32): 'Be kind and compassionate to one another, forgiving each other, just as in Christ God forgave you.' If this expression of the fruit of the Spirit is to be exercised to all, how much more should it be exercised within the context of Christian marriages? Richard Steele writes: 'Let some lesser faults be winked at, and let the husband look for a better time to discreetly admonish his wife, and the wife respectfully acquaint the husband with things amiss.'[5] When we look on the horizon of our relationship with our spouse, and see a potential conflict looming large, we will be well served in reflecting on the words of the writer of the Proverbs, 'Better a patient man than a warrior, a man who controls his temper than one who takes a city' (Prov. 16:32). One of the greatest ways we will give expression to 'learning to die daily while we are living' is letting go of our sense of entitlement, humbly setting aside our sense of what we perceive to be our rights, recognizing that all that we have and all that we are is a gracious extension of God's undeserved goodness to us.

That brings us to a fourth duty to be carried out toward one another, still growing out of our identity in Christ. *Look for, and labor toward, the certainty of your spouse's salvation.* In Hebrews 3:13, we read 'encourage one another daily, so that none of you may be hardened by sin's deceitfulness'. Obviously, this command is directed at the church in general. But where can (and should) this command be fulfilled more effectively than in the context of a marriage and Christ-centered home?

William Perkins would see this as the means to fulfilling one of four primary duties in preparing to die well: to make certain that you truly possess eternal life. He reminds us of what Paul commands in 2 Corinthians 13:5: 'Examine yourselves to see whether you are in the faith; test yourselves. Do you not realize that Christ Jesus is in you – unless, of course, you fail the test?'

By inference, we see in Scripture that those who are *in the faith* are those who *walk by faith.*

Some time ago I preached a series of sermons on Habakkuk 2:4, where the prophet writes, 'the righteous shall live by faith.' The implications of this statement are numerous and far-reaching, but can also be summarized by the following seven aspects of living by faith.

1) Living by faith is the essential effect of Christ living in me: 'I have been crucified with Christ and I no longer live, but Christ lives in me. The life I live in the body, I live by faith in the Son of God, who loved me and gave himself for me' (Gal. 2:20).

---

[5] Ibid., p. 278.

2) Living by faith is the necessary prerequisite to understanding: 'By faith we understand that the universe was formed at God's command, so that what is seen was not made out of what was visible' (Heb. 11:3).

3) Living by faith gives expression to the fear of God and results in obedience: 'By faith Noah, when warned about things not yet seen, in holy fear built an ark to save his family' (Heb. 11:7).

4) Living by faith reminds us that we are citizens of heaven, living temporarily in an earthly foreign country: 'By faith he made his home in the promised land like a stranger in a foreign country; he lived in tents, as did Isaac and Jacob, who were heirs with him of the same promise' (Heb. 11:9).

5) Living by faith empowers willing obedience, even when the details and outcome remain uncertain: 'By faith Abraham, when called to go to a place he would later receive as his inheritance, obeyed and went, even though he did not know where he was going' (Heb. 11:8).

6) Living by faith emboldens us to attempt the impossible, and even what to others may appear absurd! 'By faith Abraham, even though he was past age – and Sarah herself was barren – was enabled to become a father because he considered him faithful who had made the promise' (Heb. 11:11).

7) Living by faith keeps one eye always fixed on the horizon. It takes the long view and thinks long term. 'All these people were still living by faith when they died. They did not receive the things promised; they only saw them and welcomed them from a distance' (Heb. 11:13).

These are the experiential aspects which we seek to identify in our lives as we 'examine ourselves to see whether we are in the faith'.

What greater service could we provide to the one whom God has given us to complete us and to share the joys and frustrations of this life with us, than to look for, and labor toward, the certainty of that one's eternal salvation. Richard Steele adds: 'Your curtain-talk should often be of God, and of your eternal estate, and you should improve that analogy which is between Christ and his church and the married couple, to your comfort and direction.'[6] 'Curtain talk' is what we would call 'behind closed doors conversation'. From

---

[6] Ibid., p. 279.

the perspective of the Puritan writers, even the bedroom is a place where we are to take opportunity to direct our conversation, and vision, toward eternity.

The fifth duty to be carried out toward one another, still growing out of our identity in Christ, is to uphold one another's reputation. Richard Steele writes: 'If you are really one, and not two, the husband cannot be sick or grieving without the wife also partaking in the sickness or grief. One's reputation cannot be damaged without the other's also. The reputation of the wife the husband must tender *(protect)* as the apple of his eye; and the wife must, in every way, advance the good name of her husband. Nothing but death will separate their affections or interests.'[7] This is inseparably linked with seeking one another's contentment in the context of marriage. Paul implies this in 1 Corinthians 7:33-34: 'a married man is concerned about the affairs of this world – *how he can please his wife* – and his interests are divided.... a married woman is concerned about the affairs of this world – *how she can please her husband.*' If the husband/wife relationship was created, in part, to present a fitting picture of the relationship between Christ and the church, then the husband and wife must both be committed to striving toward one another's contentment and mutual satisfaction, and toward displaying a relationship in which the character of Christ is evidenced with integrity. This will happen only as both the husband and wife strive toward ever-increasing godly character, earning and protecting the godly reputation that such character produces.

Finally, if the identity of the godly husband and wife is wrapped up in their being redeemed and restored to a right relationship with the God from whom their sin had separated them, then their highest privilege is to be a couple devoted to prayer: enjoying the richness of his fellowship in communion with him. Few activities hold greater potential in the Christian marriage and family than learning to *enjoy* praying together as a couple and as a family. The apostle Peter writes, 'Husbands, be considerate as you live with your wives and treat them with respect as the weaker partner and as co-heirs with you of the gracious gift of life, so that nothing will hinder *your* (plural) prayers' (1 Pet. 3:7). At the same time,

---

[7] Ibid., pp. 280-81.

I'm convinced that one of the chief reasons most men and women are uncomfortable praying in public is because they're not praying with their spouse and children as part of their daily routine. If you love your spouse, the greatest expressions of that love are those that impact upon eternity, of which worship and prayer are the most important. Richard Steele wrote: 'The purest love is written in prayer. This duty must be constantly done for and with each other. There is no better preservative of real love and peace than praying together.'[8] This will be expanded in much greater detail in later chapters.

We end where we began: few things more attractively display and persuasively commend the glory of God in the life of a Christian than a Christ-centered marriage and the Christ-centered family relationships that grow out of that marriage. When we learn to relate to our family members with the theme of *memento mori* ringing in our ears, we are given the freedom to serve one another with an eager anticipation of what is being produced and secured in the lives of those we love. Then, as we learn to recognize every part of our God-given roles as an extension of our privilege rather than a potential infringement upon our rights, we gain the ever-increasing capacity to celebrate our identity in Christ as we serve. And as our understanding of the roles to which he has called us is undergirded by the assurance of the eternal privilege that awaits us, we are progressively led deeper into a life of worship. Only in this way will we attractively display and persuasively commend the glory of God through our lives, as we humbly recognize that everything we have and all that we are is a gift from the One who calls us by his grace, for his glory.

QUESTIONS FOR FURTHER STUDY AND REFLECTION

1. Under whose authority are you called to live in submission? (Rom. 10:3; 13:1-5; 1 Cor. 16:15-16; Heb. 13:17)

2. What is the only means of faithfully living in submission to the authority God has placed over you? (Eph. 5:18)

3. Are you positively and patiently affirming the dignity of those in your family who, like you, have been created in the image of God? (Gen. 1:27)

---

[8] Ibid., p. 281.

4. Are you allowing God to use you as an instrument of grace in the life of the one he has called you to complete? (Gen. 2:18-25)

5. Is the grace of God evident in your marriage as you and your spouse faithfully fulfill the mutual duties to which God has called you? (Eph. 4:1-2, 32)

3

The Role of the Husband
in the Godly Family

I remember the day well. I was sitting on the couch in the apartment we lived in during my last year of seminary. I was determined to finish reading one of the required texts for a class I was taking on pastoral ethics. Knowing that material from this book would appear on the final exam, I carefully highlighted what I felt were the salient points. I was pleased with the progress I had made that afternoon, having read and highlighted well over one hundred pages. Just then, my wife walked through the room carrying an armload of laundry. 'Whatcha doin'?' she asked with a curious smile. I felt that what I was doing should have been obvious to her, so with a less-than-gracious tone I replied, 'What's it look like I'm doing?' Bad answer. Amy never slowed her step. She just kept walking, laundry and all. But as she turned the corner into the hallway, she glanced at me and said, with a slightly condescending smile, 'Looks to me like you're highlighting all that really important stuff with your son's new disappearing ink pen.'

The truth, and its implications, slowly dawned on me as we began laughing together. That morning, a new box of Rice Crispies cereal had been opened, on which was written, 'FREE! Disappearing Ink Pen!' Unfortunately, that yellow marker, which brought much delight to our children, looked amazingly like my other felt-tipped markers, so much so that I grabbed it from the kitchen counter instead of the one I had used the day before. You cannot imagine the shock, and then dismay, that swept over me as I flipped back over the pages I had read that day. The further back

I turned, the fainter the neon yellow highlighter ink was, and the pages with which I had begun that day showed no traces of yellow whatsoever. It had vanished entirely!

The pages of the book I read that day are much like our minds. Many words, experiences, and images cover the pages of our minds. Some, for a variety of reasons, stand out more clearly than others, and it is these that we highlight. We record them with indelible ink, so that they are never forgotten, regardless of how much time goes by. Other things we record on the pages of our minds with disappearing ink. Those things seem so fresh and clear when we imprint them, but before much time passes, they begin to fade from memory. Ultimately they are forgotten completely.

What makes this a significant and real concern to each of us is our natural tendency to use the wrong kind of ink. It's been said, using slightly different imagery, that we write our disappointments in stone, but our blessings we write in dust for the winds of time to blow away. The memories of places we've met with disappointment and pain can be recalled with amazingly vivid accuracy. We remember the words that were spoken with cutting intent. We remember promises made that filled us with anticipation and hope, yet covered us with despair when they remained unfulfilled. A few notes of a song can immediately launch the recollection of an image or experience so real that even after many years our hearts begin to ache.

We write, even chisel, our disappointments in stone... but our blessings we write in dust. It's like recording your gratitude for God's goodness and faithfulness to you with your finger in the dust upon the sill beneath an open window. Your gratitude would be initially reflected, but only for a short time. As the winds of time continue to blow, gently or fiercely, old dust would be replaced with new, and your recollections of that gratitude would become increasingly distant and dim. You've recorded what God has graciously done in your life with disappearing ink, and the results are not only disheartening, they are destructive.

This is the springboard to understanding what the Puritans generally taught as being the primary responsibility of the husband and father in the godly home. This isn't immediately evident, since much of their writing centers on the clear command for husbands to love their wives. Yet as we consider the nature and expression of this love, we'll come to see more clearly why this emphasis on right remembering is critical to the role of the godly husband, especially as he labors to fulfill his greatest responsibility – that of preparing each member of his family for eternity. *Memento mori.*

In Ephesians 5:25-29, Paul writes these words:

> Husbands, love your wives, just as Christ loved the church and gave himself up for her to make her holy, cleansing her by the washing with water through the word, and to present her to himself as a radiant church, without stain or wrinkle or any other blemish, but holy and blameless. In this same way, husbands ought to love their wives as their own bodies. He who loves his wife loves himself. After all, no one ever hated his own body, but he feeds and cares for it, just as Christ does the church.

A clear pattern for the husband's love for his wife (and children) emerges in two parts from these verses. The first is based upon a theological perspective; the second is personal.

The theological perspective with which Paul begins is an impossible one for us to embrace on a merely human level, for he says in verse 25, 'Husbands, love your wives, just as Christ loved the church.' The words 'just as' are what make this command humanly impossible, for no one, in their own strength, can do anything just as Christ did. This entire passage is designed to point us to our deep need for divine grace to enable us to do, and even desire, what is otherwise impossible. This becomes glaringly evident in the imagery Paul uses to describe the unique character of Christ's love for the church.

Christ loves the church in a *supernatural* way. He loved freely: 'just as Christ loved the church and *gave* himself up for her... *cleansing* her' (vv. 25-26). The fact that Christ *gave* in order to *cleanse* his bride speaks volumes. Often we are willing to give of ourselves in order to gain something of far greater value. But Christ gave in order to *cleanse* his bride, indicating the condition in which he found her: filthy and soiled. In other words, the Lord Jesus wasn't asking, 'What's in it for me?' when he gave himself for us. He chose to love us before there was anything lovely or lovable in us at all!

When the Lord took my first wife home, I felt that I had enjoyed all that this life could ever offer in terms of the love of a godly wife.

I never expected to love another the way I had grown to love Amy. But then the most amazing thing happened. I slowly began to be drawn to the woman whom God had graciously provided as the nanny to care for my children. I found myself overcome by her loveliness – an inner beauty that subtly eclipsed even her striking outward beauty. She progressively brought light, joy, and color to my black-and-white world. At the same time, I quietly watched my children grow to love a woman who, to them, was absolutely lovely and lovable. I watched with even greater amazement as she grew to love them, even at those times when they weren't quite so lovable. The memories of our wedding day still fill my eyes with tears as I recall the wonder and awe I felt as I looked into the eyes of a radiant woman, and pledged to love this one whom I found to be absolutely lovely and lovable.

How different it is with our heavenly husband. Romans 5:8 says, 'But God demonstrates his own love for us in this: While we were still sinners, Christ died for us.' Christ didn't love us because we were lovely or lovable, he loved us in spite of our defilement, ugliness and rebellion. Tim Keller, one of my seminary professors, has often said, 'The truth is, we are far more sinful than we realize, yet far more loved and accepted than we ever imagined possible.' Christ loved us freely, apart from anything we had done, or ever could do.

The second aspect of Christ's love for the church which serves as the pattern for the husband's love for his wife is that it was *sacrificial*. Ephesians 5:25 says that Christ 'gave himself up for her'. He willingly died in our place, absorbing in himself the full extent of our sin's consequences. Implicit in dying for us, though, is the amazing reality that *he had to die first to his own desires before he could die for us*. In Luke 22:42, Jesus acknowledges his own desires, and then in the same sentence, expresses his willingness to die to them: 'Father, if you are willing, take this cup from me; *yet not my will*, but yours be done.' Here again, if we desire to die well in the end, we must learn to die daily while we are living. Only in this way will the fullness of Christ's life be ours.

Thirdly, Christ's love for the church was *purposeful* – it embraced the deliberate design and end of making the bride of Christ holy. Again, Ephesians 5:25-26 reminds us that 'Christ loved the church and gave himself up for her *to make her holy*'. His sacrifice of himself was not only to save us *from* the eternal penalty of our sin, but also to save us *to* the holiness which he perfectly represents and embodies. His design is to continually change us and perfect within us his own likeness.

This is the theological perspective with which Paul begins in presenting the pattern of the husband's love for his wife: 'Husbands, love your wives, *just as* Christ loved the church.' It is the husband's role, by God's design, to love his wife (and children) freely, sacrificially, and purposefully. Clearly, apart from God's enabling grace, no husband can ever hope to measure up to this pattern. But since God never calls us to a specific role without also enabling us to fulfill the duties and responsibilities within that role, we must affirm that this is what God expects of the Christian husband and father.

For this reason, a Christian husband must chisel in stone a clear understanding that his love for his wife is never contingent on her loveliness or lovability. He is commanded to love her as Christ loved the church, even when she is at the extreme of being rebellious and unattractive. The husband has been called to love her sacrificially, being willing to die to his own desires, that he may be diligent to meet and satisfy hers. He has been called to love her purposefully, always remembering that he will one day be required to give an account of his faithfulness in seeking to encourage the character of Christ within her.

The pattern of Christ's love for the church consistently displays a forward-looking perspective. It anticipates an eternal future and demands an eternal perspective in every area of life. First John 3:2-3 says, 'Dear friends, now we are children of God, and what we will be has not yet been made known. But we know that when he appears, we shall be like him, for we shall see him as he is. Everyone who has this hope in him purifies himself, just as he is pure.' The Puritans understood the exercise of a Christ-like love as being the practical expression of purifying ourselves and participating in the purifying of those for whom we are responsible in our families. Further, they understood the exercise of a Christ-like love as being the necessary consequence of living with an expectation of Christ's return and our being conformed to his image. All of this assumes and requires a life committed to ongoing transformation – a willingness to strive for Christ-centered growth in our own lives, and a willingness to strive for Christ-centered growth in the lives of those in our families. Oh that the beauty and excellence of Christ would be ever more visible in the families that bear his name!

Some current marriage and family counseling theories emphasize that it is not ever the husband's role to change his wife. If it were so there would be little motive for accepting his wife and loving her deeply as she is. Here the Puritans applied their casuistry with even greater accuracy than many of our contemporary therapists. They taught that because the husband was to love his wife as Christ loved the church, he was to constantly point her to Christ, being an agent of sanctification in her life. As such, he became a deliberate instrument of change in her life (and she in his), again with a view toward ever-increasing Christlikeness displayed throughout the entire family.

Having presented a theological perspective on the husband's love for his wife, Paul turns his attention to a *personal perspective*. Twice in this passage, Paul declares that the husband must love his wife as he loves and cares for himself – his own body. In Ephesians 5:28 he says, 'In this same way, husbands ought to love their wives as their own bodies. He who loves his wife loves himself.' Then in Ephesians 5:33 he says, 'However, each one of you also must love his wife as he loves himself.' But how exactly does a man's love for himself become the pattern for his love for his wife? The parallels are many, but will largely fall into two categories.

First, a husband must love his wife *attentively*, as he loves himself. In Ephesians 5:29 Paul says, 'No one ever hated his own body, but he feeds and cares for it.' We tend to take special care of our bodies and give special attention to the needs, pains, or deficiencies we experience. We generally make it our practice to examine our appearance in a mirror – initially, as we begin the day, and sporadically throughout the day. The attention we give ourselves is always purposeful. We care for our bodies with a desire to correct whatever is amiss, and to eliminate whatever causes us pain.

Think, for example, of the last pair of shoes you purchased. You selected them based on their appearance (and cost), but determined to keep them based on how they felt after you tried them on. You walked in them, stared at them, wriggled your toes in them, poked and tugged at them. Based upon the attentiveness to the desire for your body's comfort, you then purchased them. You knew that if you didn't pay special attention to your feet, you would in all likelihood suffer the consequences of blisters, or worse!

The same holds true for a husband's love for his wife. He cannot simply assume that all is well with her or with their relationship. He must love her attentively, as he loves himself, or suffer the inevitable consequences that arise from inattention or neglect.

Further, it goes without saying that a man's body has special and immediate access to his own mind. If a finger is burned, the mind knows it immediately. The finger doesn't have to delay informing the mind until an appropriate time, nor is there a need for a go-between to inform the mind of what is obvious to the finger. Richard Steele has written, 'A woman should need no mediator to her husband, for he should have his ear open to her, as well as his hand, and his heart, ready to pity, help, and gratify her, even as he is ready to help himself.'[1]

Second, a husband must love his wife *tenderly*, as he loves himself. Again, Ephesians 5:29 may be quoted: 'No one ever hated his own body, but he feeds and cares for it, just as Christ does the church.' Do you remember the last time you were walking barefoot on a wooden deck and got a splinter in your foot? Someone may have brought a needle and offered to extract it for you. But you know what that's like! I know that if it's my foot, as soon as someone begins digging in it with a sharp instrument to extract whatever is causing pain, my immediate response is, 'Give me that needle! Let me do it!' The assumption is that no one will be as careful with my own body as I can be. Again, Richard Steele said in this connection, 'No one can handle a man's sores as tenderly as himself.'[2] This is the imagery behind the husband's love for his wife. He must graciously and attentively recognize her weaknesses, anxieties or deficiencies, and help her address them as tenderly as if they were his own.

This pattern of love gives rise to various forms of expression within the context of the godly marriage and home. In general, the Puritans identified that expression with the same terminology as is used to describe Christ's expression of love in redeeming his church. The twenty-third question of the Westminster

---

[1] *Puritan Sermons, 1659–1689*, Vol.2 (1674. Reprint, Wheaton, Ill: Richard Owen Roberts Publishers, 1981), p. 286.

[2] Ibid., p. 285.

Shorter Catechism asks, 'What offices does Christ execute as our Redeemer?' It answers, 'Christ, as our Redeemer, executes the offices of a prophet, of a priest, and of a king, both in his state of humiliation and exaltation.' The conclusion, therefore, is that the husband is to love his wife as Christ loved the church – as a prophet, priest, and king.

The twenty-fourth question of the Shorter Catechism addresses the role of the prophet: 'How does Christ execute the office of a prophet?' The answer: 'Christ executes the office of a prophet in revealing to us, by his word and Spirit, the will of God for our salvation.' If the husband is to love his wife as Christ loved the church, then he's been called to demonstrate that love as he functions as the prophet of his home. He does so by revealing to his wife and family the will of God for their salvation as it is revealed in God's word by his Spirit. He has been called to be a herald of truth within his home. He has been charged to be the mouthpiece through which the voice of God is heard in his home.

From a proactive perspective this means the husband is to diligently and faithfully instruct his family in the knowledge of and desire for truth. He must consistently set the standard, not only in practice, but also by the spoken word. Many husbands and fathers feel that as long as they set a faithful example of moral behavior, they have discharged their duty. But too often the example that is set ignores the need for the verbal expression of why this example is right and on what it is based. If I as a father set a godly example before my wife and children, yet don't explain the grace that enables and drives that example, then I set them up for failure. Richard Steele wrote, 'A man can show no greater mark of his true love for his wife than to take care that she, along with himself, worship God aright in this life, in order that they may together enjoy God in the life to come. If he neglects his endeavors, she will be likely to curse him forever in hell.'[3]

But there is also a corrective perspective, for as a prophet the husband must patiently and gently reprove his wife and family when they stray. Five times in Ezekiel's prophecy we read of the watchman's responsibility to warn those against whom he sees the sword coming. Listen to the words that were first applied to the 'shepherds' of Israel's people, but apply also to us:

[3] Ibid., p. 286.

When I say to a wicked man, 'You will surely die,' and you do not warn him or speak out to dissuade him from his evil ways in order to save his life, that wicked man will die for his sin, and I will hold you accountable for his blood (3:18).

Again, when a righteous man turns from his righteousness and does evil, and I put a stumbling block before him, he will die. Since you did not warn him, he will die for his sin. The righteous things he did will not be remembered, and I will hold you accountable for his blood (3:20).

But if the watchman sees the sword coming and does not blow the trumpet to warn the people and the sword comes and takes the life of one of them, that man will be taken away because of his sin, but I will hold the watchman accountable for his blood (33:6).

When I say to the wicked, 'O wicked man, you will surely die,' and you do not speak out to dissuade him from his ways, that wicked man will die for his sin, and I will hold you accountable for his blood (33:8).

This is what the Sovereign LORD says: I am against the shepherds and will hold them accountable for my flock. I will remove them from tending the flock so that the shepherds can no longer feed themselves. I will rescue my flock from their mouths, and it will no longer be food for them (34:10).

On one level, it should be noted that the Puritans in general were not overly critical in their exercise of the office of prophet, nor were they especially overbearing. Their perspective indicated that there needed to be moderation in correction and reproof. Richard Steele wrote, 'As he that is always using his sword will eventually make it dull, so also he that is continually reproving and correcting will have less regard given to his reproofs.'[4] Yet even so, did you notice that the proclaimer of truth is not only called to diligently instruct and faithfully correct, but is also warned against his own failure to fulfill that part of his role? Four times in the above passages, Ezekiel records, 'I will hold you accountable for his blood.' There was a great sobriety to Puritan thought in this connection. The husband simply was not free to decide for himself whether or not

---

[4] Ibid., p. 287.

he was inclined to love his family as a prophet. It was his duty, and it was to his own peril that he would ignore it! His God-given assignment was to make certain that he was the means through which the infallible Word of God was consistently brought to bear upon every aspect of his family's experience.

Larry Crabb, in his book *The Silence of Adam*, sheds even further light on this part of the husband's role. He looks back at Genesis 2 and notes that when God created man and woman, it was to Adam alone that he gave the prohibition against eating from the tree of the knowledge of good and evil (vv. 16-18). The woman had not even been created at this point! From this perspective, Genesis 3:1-6 takes on new meaning:

> Now the serpent was more crafty than any of the wild animals the LORD God had made. He said to the woman, 'Did God really say, "You must not eat from any tree in the garden"?'
>
> The woman said to the serpent, 'We may eat fruit from the trees in the garden, but God did say, "You must not eat fruit from the tree that is in the middle of the garden, and you must not touch it, or you will die."'
>
> 'You will not surely die,' the serpent said to the woman. 'For God knows that when you eat of it your eyes will be opened, and you will be like God, knowing good and evil.'
>
> When the woman saw that the fruit of the tree was good for food and pleasing to the eye, and also desirable for gaining wisdom, she took some and ate it. She also gave some to her husband, who was with her, and he ate it.

Did you catch that last sentence? 'She also gave some to her husband, *who was with her,* and he ate it.' The one who alone was commanded against eating of that single tree stood silently watching his wife violate that prohibition! The text says specifically that he was there, in physical proximity to her, yet he made no effort to stop her, nor to remind her of what he had been commanded. Crabb states that Adam's greatest sin was not in eating the fruit, but in remaining silent! The Puritans would have stated it this way: 'he failed to love his wife as a prophet.' The voice of God was not heard from his lips.[5]

---

[5] Crabb, Larry, *The Silence of Adam* (Grand Rapids, MI: Zondervan, 1995), p. 79.

God created man to be a prophet, and to love his wife and family as a prophet, to remember the truth of God, and to proclaim that truth in a world that is in desperate need of it.

Tragedy struck for Adam, and it will strike for us, when we fail to do what we were created to do and when we fail to love as we were created to love.

There are logical questions that need to be asked here: How many words of Scripture have passed your lips this past week in your home? How many times have your wife or children heard you say, 'Let's pray together about that,' in response to their various expressions of concern? How many times has the question, 'What should I do?' led you to ask, 'What would most clearly display God's glory?' How many times have you reminded your family of what God has done in your past to encourage and embolden them in the present?

Remember what Moses, as a prophet, said to his people as they were preparing to enter the promised land:

> When Moses finished reciting all these words to all Israel, he said to them, 'Take to heart all the words I have solemnly declared to you this day, so that you may command your children to obey carefully all the words of this law. They are not just idle words for you – *they are your life*' (Deut. 32:45-47).

If we fail here, tragedy will strike. And that tragedy will begin as it did for Adam: with blaming those we love most for our own failure.

When God asked Adam, 'Who told you that you were naked? Have you eaten from the tree that I commanded you not to eat from?', Adam ignored the question. He first blamed the woman, and then he blamed God for putting the woman there in the first place: 'The woman you put here with me – she gave me some fruit from the tree, and I ate it' (Gen. 3:12). From the very beginning, the godly husband's duty began with loving his wife and children as a prophet – to bring the living Word of God to bear upon his family's experience. To fail here inevitably brings failure in every other dimension of the life of his family. You must proclaim what Adam did not: if you eat of this tree, remember that you must die: *memento mori*.

In loving his wife as Christ loved the church, the husband is called, secondly, to love her as a priest. The twenty-fifth question of the Shorter Catechism addresses that role: 'How does Christ execute the office of a priest?' The answer: 'Christ executes the office of Priest in his once offering up of himself a sacrifice to satisfy divine justice and reconcile us to God, and in making continual intercession for us.'

There are two components to that answer: *sacrifice* and *prayer*. Both are critical to the faithful exercise of the husband's duty in loving his wife and family. In Ephesians 5:25-27, Paul writes:

> Husbands, love your wives, just as Christ loved the church and gave himself up for her to make her holy, cleansing her by the washing with water through the word, and to present her to himself as a radiant church, without stain or wrinkle or any other blemish, but holy and blameless.

Throughout all the imagery of Christ's loving the church and giving himself for her is his willingness to sacrifice – to die to his own desire for comfort and ease and to live for the eternal benefit of his own.

Ultimately, Christ's willingness to sacrifice was what lay at the heart of satisfying divine justice. The righteous demands of God's justice could not be set aside. Nor could God say, 'Let's just forget about your sin – I forgive you.' The wrath of God had to be poured out against our sin – either in us or in Christ. He took our sin upon himself. In a similar way, the husband's willingness to sacrifice in loving his wife and family carries a divine perspective. He doesn't sacrifice to satisfy *divine justice*. Rather, he loves with a willingness to sacrifice whatever is necessary for the eternal benefit of his wife and family in order to fulfill *divine responsibility*. As Christ took the initiative in securing reconciliation between us and the God from whom our sin had separated us, so the godly husband must be willing to sacrifice by taking the initiative in seeking forgiveness and in pursuing reconciliation with those for whom he is responsible.

This self-sacrificing love is pictured again in Galatians 2:20, where Paul writes, 'I have been crucified with Christ and I no longer live, but Christ lives in me. The life I live in the body, I live by faith in the Son of God, who loved me and gave himself for me.'

The Christ who lives in me first gave himself for me. The life I now live, therefore, is lived by faith in him, as an ongoing expression of that willingness to sacrifice.

One of the most challenging areas in which this willingness to sacrifice is to be expressed is *patience*. This comes naturally to few. Patience is where the authenticity of our willingness to sacrifice for the benefit of those we love is put to the test. Yet it is here that the godly husband must take the initiative, rather than being content to be reciprocal in patience – that is, to be patient only when others around us are patient. Again, our Great High Priest is our example in this. Hebrews 4:15 says, 'For we do not have a high priest who is unable to sympathize with our weaknesses, but we have one who has been tempted in every way, just as we are – yet was without sin.'

As a priest, the godly husband loves his wife and family through the exercise of a willingness to sacrifice for them. But the other primary aspect of a priest's role is to lead those for whom he is responsible to the throne of grace. His duty is to take the initiative toward establishing and maintaining a practice of communion with God. Hebrews 10:19-22 says,

> Therefore, brothers, since we have confidence to enter the Most Holy Place by the blood of Jesus, by a new and living way opened for us through the curtain, that is, his body, and since we have a great priest over the house of God, let us draw near to God with a sincere heart in full assurance of faith, having our hearts sprinkled to cleanse us from a guilty conscience and having our bodies washed with pure water.

Since redemption has been fully accomplished and all the righteous demands of God's justice have been fully satisfied, we now have unrestricted and intimate access to the presence of our Heavenly Father. This access is not through a system nor by a procedure, but in a person – Jesus Christ himself. Therefore, since this new and living way has been opened to us, we are offered the high privilege of *drawing near*.

But is this *drawing near* a privilege designed primarily for individuals? Most of our current discipleship materials emphasize the value and importance of a disciplined prayer life – primarily in faithful personal daily devotions or quiet times. But if we were to look back at what daily time with our Creator looked like before the fall, we would find that God came to the garden in the cool of the evening to meet with Adam and Eve *together*. He didn't say, 'Adam, wait here while Eve and I walk over yonder and talk together for a while, and then later you and I can visit together by ourselves.' No, the man and woman, whom God had brought together in perfect union with one another, spent time *together* in God's presence. After all, this is the God who said, 'It is not good for man to be alone' and then made a helper suitable for him to complete him – and then declared his creative work 'very good'. Would not God then take greatest pleasure in meeting with the man and woman together?

This, I believe, is one of the most neglected privileges offered to God's redeemed people. A husband and wife have the incredible privilege of uniting their hearts and minds in a unique and powerful way as they daily enter God's presence together in prayer. By this means, our gracious God offers to redeemed couples a spiritual intimacy that nothing else in this life even begins to approach. And yet how few husbands and wives have discovered this treasure! I'm amazed at how many Christian couples, regardless of how long they've been married, simply do not pray together. They claim their schedules do not allow for it, or they don't know how, or even that they're embarrassed to do so. But consider carefully the tremendous offer of deeper spiritual intimacy that is being sacrificed by an unwillingness to go to the throne of grace together. If our Father in heaven graciously offers us this intimacy with himself and with each other, then it is clearly the godly husband's duty to take the initiative in faithfully leading his wife and family to the throne room of God's presence.

Finally, there is the third office in which Christ loves the church – that of a king. By this example, therefore, the godly husband is called to love his wife, and his family, as a king. The natural response is that the role of a king would be the easiest for any husband to fulfill. But the twenty-sixth question of the Shorter Catechism addresses this role in this way: 'How does Christ execute the office of a king?' The answer: 'Christ executes the office of King in subduing us to himself, and in ruling and defending us and in restraining and conquering all his and our enemies.' Clearly this indicates duties that go far beyond a headship that simply means being 'king of the hill'. The headship of a king carries significant responsibilities that may not be immediately obvious.

First, the husband must exercise authority over those who have been entrusted to him. But that authority must be exercised as Christ exercises his authority over the church: graciously, compassionately, and mercifully. Christ doesn't rule over his people with an iron fist. As our Creator and Redeemer he has every right to make any demands of us he wishes, for after all, we belong to him entirely. Paul says in 1 Corinthians 6:19-20: 'You are not your own; you were bought with a price. Therefore honor God with your body.' Yet in a way that more fully displays his power and authority, our Lord Jesus graciously condescends to *inviting* our submission. He causes our submitting to his authority to produce such richness, satisfaction, and security within us, that our hearts progressively relinquish the desire to be our own final authority. The great invitation and command of Christ, therefore, is to *come*. 'Come to me, all you who are weary and burdened, and I will give you rest. Take my yoke (the symbol of submission) upon you and learn from me, for I am gentle and humble in heart, and you will find rest for your souls. For my yoke is easy and my burden is light (Matt. 11:28-30).

This is the manner in which the husband, who loves his wife and family as a king, is called to follow the example of Christ. He doesn't need to rule with an iron fist. He doesn't need to repeat, 'I'm the king! I'm the king!' He exercises his God-given authority graciously, compassionately, and mercifully. Humbly acknowledging God's gracious authority over him, he invites willing submission from those entrusted to his care, and they respond joyfully, knowing that he will do what is best to provide all that they need as he loves them as Christ loves the church.

Secondly, as he loves his wife as a king, the husband defends, comforts, and encourages her. A king may rule over his kingdom only as long as he ensures that his borders are secure, and his walls have not been breached. If his kingdom is attacked and the enemy infiltrates his domain, his authority is compromised. He must then either share his authority with the enemy or lose that authority entirely. This is why the king must faithfully defend his family. His capacity to rule extends only so far and as long as he faithfully defends his own.

But how does he defend? Through truth! He faithfully reminds those in his home of the unchanging truth of God's Word; he faithfully calls into question all that is inconsistent with that truth; and he diligently labors to lead those in his home to progressively take personal ownership of that truth for themselves.

So how carefully have you been defending your kingdom? What television shows or videos do you allow in your home as 'harmless entertainment'? What books and magazines are being read in your home? What values have been embraced by the members of your family? How do they see you spending your time and money? In what way is your investment of yourself and your resources challenging them to view eternity? The consistent and relentless emphasis on truth is where comfort and encouragement begin as the husband and father loves his family as a king.

The third way a husband loves his wife and family as a king is by providing for their needs. The Puritans elevated the husband's role in this respect from being simply a breadwinner to that of being a king. They understood that a monarch was not only privileged to reap the benefits of prosperity in his kingdom, but was also expected to take responsibility for meeting the needs of those suffering from want or need. In times of famine, all eyes would look to the hand of the king for generosity. In times of uncertainty, all ears would be attentive to the words of the king for wisdom and direction. In times of danger, all hands would be raised to the power of the king for protection and deliverance. Whatever the crisis or need, the husband, who loves his wife and children as a king, is the one to whom those in his home will look.

Paul's words in 1 Timothy 5:8 need, therefore, to be applied to their full range, 'If anyone does not provide for his family, he has denied the faith and is worse than an unbeliever.' Too often even a Christian father draws the conclusion that Paul is here referring merely to providing for the *material* needs of one's family, but this does not go far enough. Paul is referring to the denial of the faith of one who does not provide for the entire range of his family's needs – *physical, emotional, and spiritual.* No king could remain secure on his throne, assured of the blessing of God upon his kingdom, if he were aware of unmet needs within his kingdom, yet content to turn a blind eye and a deaf ear. No father should expect the blessing of God on his family unless he is diligently seeking to identify all the needs of those in his home, and is faithfully embracing and offering the grace of God in response.

Finally, in loving his wife as a king, a husband must *trust* his wife. A king cannot oversee and manage an entire kingdom alone. He must delegate authority to those who will faithfully co-labor with him in the responsibility of leadership, then he must trust those to whom he's delegated that authority. In much the same way, the husband must not only trust his wife to exercise the authority entrusted to her, but must allow her the freedom to co-labor with him in the manner that most effectively employs the unique gifts and abilities God has entrusted to her. Proverbs 31:11 says of the woman of virtue, 'Her husband has full confidence in her and lacks nothing of value.' A godly husband will recognize the unique gifts and qualities of his wife, and will trust and encourage her to develop her ability to effectively use what God has entrusted to her.

Clearly, the husband who loves his wife and family in a manner consistent with how Christ, our king, loved the church does not simply preside as king of the hill. His role is one of authority with accountability before God. Therefore, he is careful to exercise that authority graciously, compassionately, and mercifully, inviting submission that does not need to be demanded. Only in this way will he lead those in his home to discover and enjoy the richness, satisfaction, and security that God intended us to find in the context of being a covenant family.

If we are committed to the assertion that few things more attractively display and persuasively commend the glory of God in the life of a Christian than a Christ-centered marriage and the Christ-centered family relationships that grow out of that marriage, then we must affirm that the husband's practice of loving his wife and family must reflect the roles of prophet, priest, and king. As a prophet, he listens carefully to God's voice, with a view toward remembering, teaching, and encouraging obedience to a right understanding of God's will. As a priest, his life expresses a willingness to sacrifice for those in his home, and a determination to lead each one to the throne of grace in worship and prayer. As a king, he exercises and delegates authority, as he maintains the security and stability of the home he's been called to defend, and for which he's been called to provide. In each respect, he must be diligent to pursue truth, to remember truth, to proclaim truth, and to lead each one in his home to embrace that truth for themselves.

QUESTIONS FOR FURTHER STUDY AND REFLECTION

1. How clearly does your love for your wife represent Christ's love for the church? (Eph. 5:25-27)

2. Are you loving your wife and family as a prophet, faithfully proclaiming the truth, with integrity, before their watching eyes and listening ears? (Ezek. 33:6; Deut. 32:45-47)

3. How many words of Scripture have passed your lips this past week as you've spoken to those in your home? How many times have your wife or children heard you say, 'Let's pray together about that'? How many times have you reminded your family of what God has done in your past to encourage and embolden them in the present? (Ps. 44:1-3)

4. Are you loving your wife and family as a priest, faithfully exercising the leadership role in your family as you display self-sacrificing love, patience, compassion, gentleness, and humility? (Col. 3:12-14)

5. Are you faithfully taking the initiative in leading your family toward seeking forgiveness for the continued sin in your life and theirs? (Heb. 4:16; 1 John 1:9)

6. Are you loving your wife and family as a king, exercising gracious and compassionate authority, as you lead, encourage, trust, and provide for their needs?

7. Do you bring security and stability to your home, or do you detract from it?

4

THE ROLE OF THE WIFE
IN THE GODLY FAMILY

Not long ago, the Southern Baptist Convention met and deliberated over a wide variety of issues that were relevant to the life and ministry of their denomination at that time. While the various media reported on the convention in general, nothing received more press than the denomination's reaffirmation of the Biblical command for the wife to live in submission to her husband. Some of the reports simply reflected the denomination's position as a statement of human interest. But most reports were critical – resoundingly so! The general consensus was that no wife should be required to submit to her husband. Any view that requires submission is antiquated, abusive, and absurd. Rather than presenting a carefully thought out argument against a wife's submission, the Biblical view was scoffed at and promptly dismissed as irrelevant. It was argued, if a wife's role is viewed as being subordinate to her husband's, then she must logically be viewed as being inferior to him – and that simply cannot be true.

Here again, the Puritans are incisively helpful. We've already seen in their writings that the Biblical model affirms the absolute equality of the husband and wife in terms of their *identity*. They are both created in the image of God, yet both reflect the utter depravity of a sinful nature. The real issue, therefore, is not identity, but *role*.

It is to this end that Paul writes in Ephesians 5:22, 'Wives, submit to your husbands as to the Lord.' Yet his statement follows immediately after verse 21, 'Submit *to one another* out of reverence for Christ.' On a merely human level, none of this is possible for us apart from the ongoing transforming work of the Holy Spirit who indwells and empowers us. By nature, each of us rebels against the Biblical command to be submissive to the authority under which God has placed us. Each of us needs what Paul commands in the introductory words to this passage: 'be filled with the Spirit' (Eph. 5:18).

Yet Paul's argument recognizes that as created beings, our identity is wrapped up in the fact that *every one* of us has been designed to line up under, and submit to, the authority of Christ, the Creator and Redeemer of the church. Every one of us will be required to give an account of our willingness (or lack thereof) to submit to the human authority that Christ has established for his redeemed people. Again, *memento mori* is a fitting reminder that it is not *our* sense of the propriety of submission in marriage that drives our willingness to embrace this design. Rather, it is our expectation of being present one day with our Heavenly Husband as he calls us home to take our place as his eternal bride. Armed with this perspective, we are filled with a joyful willingness to give expression to our identity in Christ in a way that embraces Biblical humility and submissiveness. And in so doing, we will display and commend the glory of Christ before a watching and listening world.

How then can a wife's duty to live in submission to her husband be viewed as an expression of her high privilege? The answer begins with wrestling through the New Testament passages that speak of the nature of her submission. They are as follows:

> Wives, submit to your husbands as to the Lord. For the husband is the head of the wife as Christ is the head of the church, his body, of which he is the Savior. Now as the church submits to Christ, so also wives should submit to their husbands in everything (Eph. 5:22-24).

> Wives, submit to your husbands, as is fitting in the Lord (Col. 3:18).

> A woman should learn in quietness and full submission. I do not permit a woman to teach or to have authority over a man; she must be silent. For Adam was formed first, then Eve. And Adam was not the one deceived; it was the woman who was deceived and became a sinner (1 Tim. 2:11-14).

Likewise, teach the older women to be reverent in the way they live, not to be slanderers or addicted to much wine, but to teach what is good. Then they can train the younger women to love their husbands and children, to be self-controlled and pure, to be busy at home, to be kind, and to be subject to their husbands, so that no one will malign the word of God (Titus 2:3-5).

Wives, in the same way be submissive to your husbands so that, if any of them do not believe the word, they may be won over without words by the behavior of their wives, when they see the purity and reverence of your lives. Your beauty should not come from outward adornment, such as braided hair and the wearing of gold jewelry and fine clothes. Instead, it should be that of your inner self, the unfading beauty of a gentle and quiet spirit, which is of great worth in God's sight. For this is the way the holy women of the past who put their hope in God used to make themselves beautiful. They were submissive to their own husbands, like Sarah, who obeyed Abraham and called him her master. You are her daughters if you do what is right and do not give way to fear (1 Pet. 3:1-6).

In each of these passages, the fundamental emphasis on sub-mission in no way indicates *inferiority*. Rather, the primary emphasis affirms that the wife is under her husband's authority – a spiritually-focused authority under which she has been placed by God in his gracious redemptive design. The duties, then, that each is called to fulfill in the context of the godly family are rightly viewed as an extension of the high privilege that is received with humble gratitude, and exercised with humble dependence. Again, as John Chrysostom has said, 'If they (the husband and wife) perform their proper duties, everything around them acquires firmness and stability.'[1]

But how is this relationship to be understood? How can there be absolute equality in identity before God, and absolute equality in fallenness from God, without there also being some measure of equality in the roles to which God has called us? To address this question, we may consider the writings of Richard Baxter, who in 1665 wrote *A Christian Directory,* a one thousand page manual

---

[1] *Puritan Sermons, 1659–1689,* Vol. 2 (1674. Reprint, Wheaton, Ill: Richard Owen Roberts Publishers, 1981), p. 303.

(the size of a large city telephone directory) on the godly practice of Christianity. In the introduction to his work he writes, 'Nothing is done well by him that begins not at home: as the man is, so is his strength, and work.'[2] He would apply these words to a woman as well as to a man: Nothing is done well by her that begins not at home: as the woman is, so is her strength, and work. Baxter carefully defends and applies this principle as he details the specific duties that pertain to each of them.

The Christian Directory includes eight pages of fine-print instructions on the mutual duties of husbands and wives toward each other. He follows with two pages, including ten specific categories of instructions pertaining to the special duties of husbands to their wives. From there he directs his attention to the specific duties of wives, devoting four pages and twelve specific categories relevant to that role. He follows this section with thirty-two questions, addressing a wide range of issues which complicate those duties, most of which pertain specifically to the wife. It appears that Baxter may have felt the wife's role and duties were more easily misunderstood or misapplied than the husband's.

Paraphrasing his words with respect to the mutuality of the exercise of their individual duties, *the wife that expects security and comfort in her relationship with her husband must be conscious of all her own duty to her husband. For though it remains his duty to be kind and faithful to her even when she doesn't prove worthy of that kindness and faithfulness, the security she desires from him and the duty she owes to him shall always go together. If she ignores her duty, the security she desires will elude her as well.*[3]

So what then is this duty which she cannot ignore, without sacrificing the security she so desperately desires? In what ways must she give expression to her submission to the spiritual headship and authority of her husband? And why is her willingness to honor God in this way essential to the strength and stability of her entire family and home? The answers to these questions lie in a Biblical understanding of the nature of this submission, its extent, and its basis.

---

[2] Baxter, Richard, *A Christian Directory*, Vol. 1 (Ligonier, PA: Soli Deo Gloria Publications, 1990), p. 3.
[3] Ibid., p. 440.

When we examined the husband's duty to love his wife we saw that the New Testament uses a number of images to describe the nature of that love. In each of these references, the image was introduced with the word 'as' – 'love their wives *as* their own bodies,' '*as* Christ loved the church,' '*as* Christ gave himself up for her,' and 'must love his wife *as* he loves himself.' The same construction is used to describe the nature of the wife's submission to her husband. In Ephesians 5:24, the apostle Paul writes, 'Wives submit to your husbands *as the church submits to Christ.*' So to understand the nature of the wife's submission to her husband, we must understand the nature of the church's submission to Christ.

The fundamental question is this: Can a Christian embrace the sacrificial love of Christ without also embracing and submitting to the headship and authority of Christ? The answer is clearly, 'No!' To gratefully embrace the sacrifice of Christ on our behalf demands that we also willingly submit to his authority. In 1 Corinthians 6:19-20 Paul says, 'Do you not know that your body is a temple of the Holy Spirit, who is in you, whom you have received from God? *You are not your own; you were bought at a price.* Therefore honor God with your body.' A Christian willingly recognizes that he or she is under the authority of the one who gave his life for his or her redemption.

While the husband does not in any way redeem his wife, he is called to love her in a manner that displays Christ's sacrificial love for the church. She, therefore, is called to submit to his headship, as the church submits to Christ. What makes this such a challenge, though, is that it is easy for a wife to joyfully embrace the sacrificial love of her husband, without willingly submitting to his headship. By nature we crave the freedom of independence and autonomy, and tend to resist, passively or aggressively, any form of a yoke of submission. We are much more likely to be self-centered or self-absorbed than submissive and deferential.

I was reminded not long ago of a conversation between a couple who had been married for several decades. They were relatively wealthy and enjoyed the trappings of the husband's successful career. On their way to the wife's high school class reunion, they stopped for gas in their new Mercedes. While the tank was filling the husband went to the restroom. When he returned he noticed his wife talking and laughing with a shabbily-attired attendant, who nervously walked away as he returned. 'Do you know him?' the husband asked as they pulled away. 'Oh, I used to date him,' she replied. With an air of superiority, the husband replied, 'You're lucky you married me. If I hadn't come along, you'd be the wife of a gas station attendant instead of the wife of a CEO.' Unimpressed, the wife coolly responded, 'If I had married him, he'd be the CEO and you'd be the gas station attendant!'

None of us is naturally inclined to defer to another, let alone *submit* to the headship of another. It's been said that within each one of us dwells the heart of a king – a heart that willingly bows before no one. Yet from a Biblical perspective, the husband has been called to honor Christ by loving his wife sacrificially, and the wife has been called to honor Christ by willingly submitting to the headship of her husband.

Implicit to this submission is the idea of honoring the one under whose headship we live. There is something hypocritical, demeaning, and even offensive about a Christian whose life does not honor Christ by submitting to his authority. We see it so clearly in others and are immediately turned off by such a person's inconsistency, applying to them the designation, 'hypocrite.' But isn't there also something hypocritical, demeaning, and offensive about a Christian woman whose words and practice don't honor her husband? We smile, nervously, at the cutting words of a cynical wife to her husband, 'A good husband needs to be strong, caring, and sensitive ... and you have all but three of those qualities.'

I always find myself a bit uneasy around a woman who is publicly critical of her husband. I'm especially disturbed and saddened by conversations among Christian women which include the words, 'If you think your husband is... *(insert critical label)*, wait till I tell you about mine!' What often goes unnoticed is that the public criticism of one who should be honored generally reflects negatively on the critic as well as the one being criticized. It devalues the authority of the one who should rightfully be honored, while it tarnishes and compromises the integrity of the critic. This applies to husbands as well as to wives. If you love and honor the one whom God has given to complete you (Gen. 2:18), then you will guard your words. Guard your speech against critical, dishonoring words spoken in anger, frustration, or even in jest. Not because there is no basis for such criticism (those with whom we live know just how much there really is to criticize.), but because it offends the gracious God who established marriage by bringing a man and a woman together and calling that union 'very good'. How dare we be critical of that unique relationship in which God has taken such great delight?

I should quickly add that this is not to say that we should never express our disapproval of what troubles us in our marriages. If there is something that needs to be addressed, by all means, deal with it! But do so with the one who may benefit from the expression of your concerns – your spouse. And do so in a spirit of honoring the one in whose life God has called you to be a gracious and compassionate instrument of sanctification. Richard Baxter wrote, 'None of their own matters, which should be kept secret, are to be made known to others. Teaching and reproving should be for the most part secret.'[4] The manner in which a Christian wife honors her husband will either confirm or destroy the credibility of the Word of God in the sight of those who make up her silent, but always observant audience!

Paul wrote to Titus, 'train the younger women to love their husbands and children, to be self-controlled and pure, to be busy at home, to be kind, and to be subject to their husbands, *so that no one will malign the word of God*' (Titus 2:4-5). Peter affirms this as well, 'Wives, in the same way be submissive to your husbands *so that, if any of them do not believe the word, they may be won over without words by the behavior of their wives, when they see the purity and reverence of your lives*' (1 Pet. 3:1-2). Richard Baxter concludes that the woman's own honor and respect among her own family and neighbors is largely consistent with the honor she demonstrates to her husband: 'Speak not of their infirmities to others behind their backs. Your husband's dishonor is also your own, and for you to dishonor him before others is your double shame.'[5]

The third component of a wife's submission to her husband that reflects the church's submission to Christ is the expression of an ever growing love for her husband. In our culture, the line between love and romance has been largely blurred, to the extent that the terms are used almost interchangeably by many. But over the course

---

[4] Ibid., p. 440.
[5] Ibid., p. 440.

of a couple's experience, the fact that becomes unmistakably clear is that *romance* is quickly pushed to the periphery – even completely crowded out by the competing demands of busy schedules. But the *love* we're called to express to one another can never be pushed to the periphery. This love must grow, develop, and deepen over time.

In Titus 2:3-4 Paul writes: 'Likewise, teach the older women to be reverent in the way they live, not to be slanderers or addicted to much wine, but to teach what is good. *Then they can train the younger women to love their husbands.*' We infer from this that loving one's husband (in the way Scripture commands) doesn't come naturally. It is a love that must be taught if it is to be expressed. A growing and deepening love is one that is trained to recognize and overcome the self-centeredness that naturally dwells within each one of us. Only as we deal radically with the remaining sin in our lives will we find the liberty to love and submit as Christ has called us.

Fourth, a wife submits to her husband as her words, actions, and affections reflect her foundational fear of God. The Puritan writers did not indicate by this that the wife was to live in fear or dread of her husband. Their emphasis was on the cautious diligence of one who seeks to avoid causing offense to her husband. One wife wrote, 'I will do my utmost to bring my husband contentment, for though I do not fear his hand, I fear his frown.'[6] In other words, if your respect for a certain individual is low, then you won't be very concerned with whether or not you disappoint that person. There is no real sense of loss in the absence of their acceptance and validation. But each of us knows what it is to respect and admire someone to such a degree that their approval becomes increasingly valuable – a parent, colleague, teacher, mentor, or coach, for example. The more you respect and love a person, the more it pains you to think of disappointing him or her – to the degree that you begin even to fear disappointing that one.

On one level, that's what it is to fear God: to love him so deeply that it pains us to think of grieving his Holy Spirit and to be so overwhelmed with his eternal power and glory that the thought of offending him, or even disappointing him, becomes reprehensible to us. This becomes a powerful motive toward ever-increasing Christlikeness, knowing that we live every moment of our lives in

---

[6] *Puritan Sermons, 1659–1689*, Vol. 2 (1674. Reprint, Wheaton, Ill: Richard Owen Roberts Publishers, 1981), p. 293.

anticipation of our Savior's words, 'Well done, good and faithful servant.'

That's how the church submits to Christ, and that's how the wife has been called to submit to her husband. In this respect, the willing submission of the wife to her husband is what arises from and preserves the free action of her own heart and will. Only in this kind of submission is there true liberty and joy.

But this leads to a deeper question. Why did God design the roles within a marriage the way that he did? Why did he ordain the wife to be submissive to the husband? This is the issue to which Paul responds as he addresses the *basis* for the wife's submission to her husband.

In 1 Corinthians 11:3, 8, he writes: 'Now I want you to realize that the head of every man is Christ, and the head of the woman is man, and the head of Christ is God.... *For* man did not come from woman, but woman from man.' Again, in 1 Timothy 2:12-13 Paul writes: 'I do not permit a woman to teach or to have authority over a man; she must be silent. *For* Adam was formed first, then Eve.' From the perspective of creation, Paul presents the wife's submission to her husband as being based upon sequence or order. The deliberate emphasis is on God's creating Adam first. This is in no way to be construed as making the wife inferior to the husband, or the woman to the man. But in terms of headship, God chose to invest special authority in the first of his human creation.

Implicit to this sequence is the fact that God gave the instructions regarding the tree of the knowledge of good and evil to Adam, not Eve, and therefore held Adam immediately responsible for their failure:

> Then the man and his wife heard the sound of the LORD God as he was walking in the garden in the cool of the day, and they hid from the LORD God among the trees of the garden. But the LORD God called *to the man*, 'Where are you?' He answered, 'I heard you in the garden, and I was afraid because I was naked; so I hid.' And he said, 'Who told you that you were naked? Have you (Adam – masculine singular verb) eaten from the tree that I commanded you not to eat from?' (Gen. 3:8-11).

From the very beginning, the husband carried the responsibility of spiritual headship – a headship to which the wife was called to submit.

The basis for the wife's submission to her husband is not limited to the order of creation. It follows all through the pattern of redemption. In Ephesians 5:22-23, Paul reflects that redemptive pattern when he writes: 'Wives, submit to your husbands as to the Lord. *For* the husband is the head of the wife as Christ is the head of the church, his body, of which he is the Savior.' As Christ is the head of the church he loved and gave himself for, so the husband is the head of the wife whom he is called to love, and for whom he is called to give himself. The basis for the wife's submission to her husband is woven all through the fabric of creation and redemption.

The logical question that flows from this understanding of the wife's submission to her husband is, 'To what extent?' How far does a wife's submission to her husband extend? Some would answer this question very simply, quoting the apostle Paul in Ephesians 5:24: 'Now as the church submits to Christ, so also wives should submit to their husbands *in everything*.' The extent of a wife's submission to her husband, therefore, is limitless. She is to submit to him in everything!

Now pause for a moment in your thinking. There is a standard response that I often hear from wives when I quote Paul's words in Ephesians 5:24. 'Don't you mean that I'm to submit to my husband in everything *only when he's loving me Biblically, as Christ loved the church*? And if he's not loving me as Christ loved the church, then I'm freed from the responsibility to submit to him in everything, right?' This makes a very good point, especially if we're arguing from the perspective of Ephesians 5:21 alone, 'Submit *to one another* out of reverence for Christ.' However, the clear teaching of Scripture is that God holds us accountable to live in obedience to the commands of his Word regardless of whether or not those around us are choosing to walk in obedience. From the perspective of our appearance before the Judge of all the earth on that great and final day, each of us is called to stand alone in obedience. Even in a godly marriage relationship, neither obedience, nor disobedience, is measured collectively.

The apostle Peter confirms this in 1 Peter 3:14-15: 'But even if you should suffer for what is right, you are blessed. Do not fear what they fear; do not be frightened. But in your hearts set apart Christ as Lord.' When a husband fails to love his wife as Christ loved the church, and she suffers because of it, she is still called to submit to his headship. Neither the husband's inability nor unwillingness to love in this way excuses the wife from her God-ordained role of submission.

Having said that, though, we need to qualify the extent of this submission by identifying the label the Puritans attached to it. We earlier examined the word 'as' with reference to the nature of the husband's love for his wife. Now notice in the following verses the word 'as' with reference to the nature of the wife's submission to her husband: 'Wives, submit to your husbands *as to the Lord*' (Eph. 5:22); 'Now *as the church submits to Christ*, so also wives should submit to their husbands in everything' (Eph. 5:24); 'Wives, submit to your husbands, *as is fitting in the Lord*' (Col. 3:18). 'As to the Lord... *as* the church submits to Christ... *as* is fitting in the Lord.' The Puritans identified the wife's submission to her husband as a *religious* submission. A submission to one's husband that grows out of, and is dependent upon, a wife's submission to Christ. Conversely, a wife who is unwilling to submit graciously to her husband, is thereby incapable of submitting to her Lord. A Christian wife who is not living in active submission to her husband is living in rebellion against God. And like all forms of rebellion, it can only lead to disappointment, misery, and ultimately, failure and defeat.

It is helpful to note that of all the times the New Testament uses the word 'submission' only one-third have reference to the wife's submission to her husband. All other references are directed to the wide range of other relationships in which a Christian is called to submit to the spiritual authority under which God has placed him or her. Consider a few examples of this broader perspective of a Christian's submission, all of which can be designated 'religious submission':

the sinful mind is hostile to God. It does not *submit to God's law*, nor can it do so (Rom. 8:7).

Since they did not know the righteousness that comes from God and sought to establish their own, they did not *submit to God's righteousness'* (Rom. 10:3).

Everyone must *submit himself to the governing authorities*, for there is no authority except that which God has established. The authorities that exist have been established by God (Rom. 13:1).

I urge you, brothers, to *submit to such as these and to everyone who joins in the work*, and labors at it (1 Cor. 16:15-16).

Obey your leaders (elders in the church) and *submit to their authority*. They keep watch over you as men who must give an account. Obey them so that their work will be a joy, not a burden, for that would be of no advantage to you (Heb. 13:17).

Submit yourselves for the Lord's sake to every authority instituted among men: whether to the king, as the supreme authority, or to governors, who are sent by him to punish those who do wrong and to commend those who do right.... Slaves, *submit yourselves to your masters* with all respect, not only to those who are good and considerate, but also to those who are harsh (1 Pet. 2:13-14, 18).

In none of these relationships is the command to submit dependent on our perception of the worthiness of the one to whom we are called to submit. Our failure to submit is never justified by the failure or deficiency of the one under whose spiritual authority God has placed us. In his book *Letters to an Unborn Child*, David Ireland writes about the self-less love and devotion of his wife. He was dying of a debilitating disease which had left him virtually unable to move, and completely unable to care for himself. An evening out with his wife would begin with her undressing, bathing, and redressing him. She would then wheel him out to the car, slide him in, fold up the chair, and put it into the trunk. Then she drove them to the restaurant. When they got there, she would reverse everything: get the chair out of the trunk, unfold it, and slide him out of the car and into the chair. She closed the trunk and pushed him into the restaurant. As they ate, she would feed him, wipe the dribble from his mouth, and then pay for the meal. She would then take him back out to the car and go through the process of getting him out of the chair and into his seatbelt.

Then when they got home, she would take him inside, undress him, clean him, and put him in bed. Finally, when she got into bed with him, she would cuddle in beside him, kiss him on the cheek and say, 'Thanks for taking me out to eat tonight. I had a wonderful evening.'[7] Our call to live in humble submission is never dependent on our perception of the worthiness of the one to whom we must submit. The God who designed us also established the relationships and roles within which we live out our lives. If we live our lives with a constant view toward eternity, and all that awaits us there, then we'll humbly and willingly submit to all that God has decreed for our best. Again, she who desires to die well in the end, must learn to die daily while she is living.

For each one of us, it is only a willingness to live our lives in submission to the authority of God's Word that provides the liberty to enjoy the fullness of what God created and redeemed us to enjoy. For the husband, submission to the authority of God's Word requires him to love his wife as Christ loved the church and gave himself for it. For the wife, submission to the authority of God's Word requires her to submit to her husband in everything. How then is a wife to live in joyful expression of Biblical submission to her husband?

In the *Christian Directory*, Richard Baxter makes several practical suggestions that impact upon the wife's ability to fulfill this role. First, make it your conscious and willing desire to submit to your husband's spiritual headship. 'Even if in your husband's softness or yieldingness he relinquishes his authority and lets you have your way, remember that God has appointed him to be your spiritual head... do not deceive yourself by giving him the title of your "spiritual head" when all along you intend to have your own way, for you are making a mockery of God's design.'[8]

Emily and I have missionary friends who were recently reflecting on their marriage, and shared with us some of the struggles they have overcome by the grace of God. When they married, she was much more spiritually mature than he, but she was certain of the work God had begun in her husband and was confident of his completing that work in him.

---

[7] Ireland, David, *Letters to an Unborn Child* (New York, NY: Harper & Rowe, 1974).

[8] Baxter, Richard, *A Christian Directory*, Vol.1 (Ligonier, PA: Soli Deo Gloria Publications, 1990), p. 440.

As a Christian wife, she spoke of the struggles involved in submitting to a man who at many points displayed less godliness than she. Her prayer became that God would lead her to submissiveness in her role as a wife, and would make her husband draw ever nearer to Christ, growing in his knowledge and love for the Lord. She spoke of different occasions when she questioned her husband's judgment, yet learned to quietly trust the Lord. In these situations she had to die to her own desires for security and control, in order to submit to her husband, even when she knew his choices and their consequences might not have been best.

In spite of not knowing what would happen or how his immaturity would affect her, she decisively chose to submit to God by submitting to her husband, trusting the Lord to overrule even his failures. She described how God used her quiet and submissive, yet prayerful, heart to progressively lead her husband toward the God-honoring role as the spiritual head of their family and home to which he had been called.

Now, years into their marriage, they are preparing for the mission field. It was startling, recently, to hear her say that her husband's commitment to Christ and his call upon their lives is now even deeper and stronger than hers. Over time, he has effectively become the pastor and shepherd of their home. In going beyond allowing her husband to be the titular head of their family, and in submitting to his role as the spiritual head of their home, she is finding the true fulfillment that God has designed for her role as a wife.

Second, the godly wife has been called to make it her conscious and willing desire to live in cheerful contentedness with all that God has designed for her role. 'It is a continual burden to a man to have an impatient, discontented wife. Many a poor man can easily bear his poverty himself, that yet is not able to bear his wife's impatience under it. It becomes far heavier than the poverty itself.'[9]

Third, make it your conscious and willing desire to subdue your passions and control your emotions. Again, paraphrasing Baxter, *The wife's greater tendency toward emotional extremes are often the common cause of the husband's anxiety, and the instability of the*

---

[9] Ibid., p. 440.

marriage. As long as the emotions are allowed to run uncontrolled, you will experience no calm, which will provoke the grief and unrest in your husband, which will provoke further emotional unrest in you. By all means, restrain the range of your passion (emotions), and keep a composed, patient mind.[10]

Fourth, make it your conscious and willing desire to govern your speech. Let your words be few and well considered before you speak them.[11] As Proverbs 10:19 says, 'When words are many, sin is not absent, but he who holds his tongue is wise.'

For all these duties, we find ourselves helpless unless we devote ourselves to laying hold of the grace and power of God in prayer. Three things the Puritans urged Christian husbands and wives to pray for in the pursuit of their calling were wisdom, humility, and uprightness of heart.[12] Wisdom is necessary to see ourselves as God sees us, and to respond to his assessment using the right words and attitudes, all in the context of right timing. Humility is necessary to agree, in brokenness before him, that his judgments are right. Humility then enables us to receive from him what is unavailable to us in our self-sufficiency. Uprightness of heart is necessary that we may continue forward with pure and righteous motives as we live to glorify and enjoy our God forever.

Finally, Paul reminds us, 'Those who marry will face many troubles in this life' (1 Cor. 7:28). Those troubles aren't arbitrary or disconnected. They generally arise, or are intensified, when either the husband or wife (or both) begin to move away from their God-given role or position. The challenge begins with remembering what God, in his infinite wisdom and grace, has ordained and established. It follows in learning to submit to him, and to the totality of what he says is ours in the exercise of the roles in which he has placed us. Submission, in this respect, then becomes an expression of what Paul commands in Romans 12:1: 'Therefore, I urge you, brothers, in view of God's mercy, to offer your bodies as living sacrifices, holy and pleasing to God – this is your spiritual act of worship.' If Christ-focused submission is the spiritual act of worship embraced by the husband and the wife,

---

[10] Ibid., p. 440.

[11] Ibid., p. 440.

[12] *Puritan Sermons, 1659–1689*, Vol. 2 (1674. Reprint, Wheaton, Ill: Richard Owen Roberts Publishers, 1981), p. 303.

then as Chrysostom has said, 'everything around them acquires firmness and stability.'[13]

QUESTIONS FOR FURTHER STUDY AND REFLECTION

1. Are you living in submission to your husband's God-given authority? (Eph. 5:22-24; Col. 3:18; 1 Tim. 2:11-14; Titus 2:3-5; 1 Pet. 3:1ff)

2. What is the Biblical basis for your submission to your husband? (1 Cor. 11:3, 8; Eph. 5:23; 1 Tim. 2:12-14)

3. Why can a wife's submission to her husband be described as 'religious submission'? (Eph. 5:22, 24; Col. 3:18; 1 Pet. 3:14)

4. How does the church's submission to Christ set the pattern for the wife's submission to her husband? (Eph. 5:24)

5. What is the result of a Christian wife's failure to live in Biblical submission to her husband? (Titus 2:5; 1 Pet. 3:1)

6. What is the only means of living in submission to your husband's authority with cheerfulness and contentedness? (Eph. 5:18)

---

[13] Ibid., p. 303.

5

FAMILY WORSHIP

Is it nothing to you whether your children are damned or saved? Is it nothing to you whether they live with the blessed, glorious God, or with cursed devils? Have you no pity for them that are flesh of your flesh? Where are the yearnings of your hearts? Dare you be guilty of the murder of their bodies? And dare you be guilty of the murder of their souls? Do not the laws of men justly hang those that do the one, and will not the laws of God righteously damn them that do the other? You fathers, and you mothers, can you look upon your graceless and Christless children, and not pity them, and weep over them, and call them to you to come and pray with you? Have you not a word to say to God for them in their hearing? Will you not call them to this duty, and let them be eye-witnesses of the tears you shed in lamenting their sinful state and misery thereby, and ear-witnesses of the requests you put up to God for their conversion?[1]

With this series of questions Samuel Davies pleads with fathers and mothers to labor decisively and tirelessly toward leading each person within their homes to meditate daily on death, and the life to come, with a view toward fostering a right relationship with the One who alone is able to assure them of eternal life. Yet he, along with a host of other Puritan preachers and writers, presented this duty not simply as a labor, but as a privilege – the highest privilege, in fact – that this life affords the child of God and family of God as

---

[1] *Puritan Sermons, 1659–1689*, Vol.2 (1674. Reprint, Wheaton, Ill: Richard Owen Roberts Publishers, 1981), p. 271.

they anticipate eternal worship in the life to come. It was from this perspective that Puritan writers often approached the subject of preparing for eternity. This seemed to be of special interest to them because no other subject was so closely related to the affections, the deepest desires and longings of the human heart, that are the root and motive of all our choices and actions.

We're told in Scripture that our eternal home in heaven will be filled with the unbroken, unceasing worship of the victorious Lamb of God seated at the right hand of God the Father. Worship will be so rich, full, engaging, and satisfying, that nothing in this life can even begin to approach that experience. Further, in 2 Corinthians 12, Paul describes in a halting, seemingly redundant, manner his vision of heaven, a vision which raises more questions than it actually answers. He says in verse 4 that he was caught up to paradise and heard 'inexpressible things, things that man is not permitted to tell.' I believe he is telling us that our minds do not have the capacity to comprehend even dimly the nature or experience of heaven; our hearts do not have the capacity to take in the glory of heaven; and especially, our language doesn't have the vocabulary to describe even remotely the reality of heaven.

Yet there is one part of our present experience that reflects, dimly at best, the wonder and glory of that heavenly experience: *worship.* Not just private worship, but primarily, corporate worship. And if, as individuals and families, we are living with the constant anticipation of one day joining in that heavenly worship, then the activity that will characterize a Christ-centered family is Christ-centered worship. A godly family will develop the practice of worshipping God together in their home. And the Puritan family gave expression and meaning to this great privilege.

The pattern for this worship is addressed in Psalm 118, where in verse 15 the psalmist writes, 'The voice of joyful shouting and salvation is in the tents of the righteous.' Can you imagine joyful shouting in a tent? Or joyful shouting in many tents? I love the way the New International Version translates this verse, '*Shouts of joy and victory resound in the tents of the righteous.*' *Resound* is probably the word that best describes what that joyful shouting must have sounded like in the tents of God's people. What were they shouting about? This verse and the following verse provide the answer: 'The LORD's right hand has done mighty things! The

LORD's right hand is lifted high; the LORD's right hand has done mighty things!' Clearly, God's amazing goodness and faithfulness had so overwhelmed them that whenever they recited the oral history of God's providence in the lives of his people, knowing smiles would spread across the faces of those tent-dwelling family members, infectious laughter would erupt, and even joyful shouting would not be contained. The people of God were celebrating the overwhelming victories wrought by their Captain of the armies of heaven. They were affirming and enjoying God's faithfulness in the past as a necessary basis for their confidence in his present and future faithfulness. '*Shouts of joy and victory resound in the tents of the righteous.*' Isn't that worship? Or better, isn't that what worship was intended to be?

To a large degree, this is what prepared my children for the illness and death of their first mother. From the time they were infants, they were exposed to the worship of God in our home, even before they were brought to worship in our local church. They grew up hearing God's Word being read in our living room, kitchen, and in their bedrooms. They were taught to memorize the promises of God's Word even before they were taught the name of their street or their telephone number. Through the Word they were introduced to the infinite wisdom, goodness, compassion, and power of the God they worshipped. They learned to sing – not only children's choruses, but the great hymns of the faith, and they sang them with joy! They learned to pray – and to trust, unswervingly, in the God they had grown to know and love through our worship of him in our home.

It didn't surprise me, then, that I never felt a need to conceal from them what was happening to their first mother, but could bring them to the hospital even to the last days of Amy's life. I still remember the sad but trusting faces of four small children, ages two, three, six, and eight, walking quietly into that room the last day they saw her living on this side of eternity. They held her feverish hands, looked into her unresponsive face, and sang to her:

> God that madest earth and heaven,
> darkness and light;
> Who the day for toil hast given,
> for rest the night;
> May thine angel guards defend us,

slumber sweet Thy mercy send us;
holy dreams and hopes attend us,
this live-long night.
Guard us waking, guard us sleeping,
and when we die,
May we all in Thy safekeeping,
all peaceful lie.
When the last dread trump shall wake us,
do not Thou, our God, forsake us,
but to reign in glory take us,
with Thee on high.

Please don't misunderstand; grief was not absent. Neither for my children, nor for me. There were places where the pain and the emptiness were so intense that I was left feeling like only a shadow of a person, emptied of all substance. My soul resonated with the words of the psalmist in Psalm 66:10-12:

For you, O God, tested us;
   you refined us like silver.
You brought us into prison
   and laid burdens on our backs.
You let men ride over our heads;
   we went through fire and water...

But because God had taught us to worship him as a family, we could affirm again and again the next words of that passage – *but you brought us to a place of abundance.* This was the effect family worship had on our family collectively. It taught us to look constantly to the living presence of the God who promises, 'Never will I leave you; never will I forsake you' (Heb. 13:5). Not even in death.

I've read that in the days of the early American pioneers, many of those heading west chose to blaze their own trails in their search for a place to call 'home'. On their journeys there were no roads, and relatively few landmarks by which to maintain their bearings. This made traveling especially difficult as they crossed the vast prairies. Lacking precise vision and direction, many miles were traveled in a meandering fashion.

Eventually, these pioneers learned that there were places where they could navigate only by looking backward at the tracks left by their own wagon wheels. In effect, they proceeded forward on the basis of the certainty of where they had been. In many respects, this is a picture of our pilgrimage as well. We don't see the end from the beginning, nor do we see what lies around the next bend in the road. But we know the One who says, 'I know the plans I have for you... plans to prosper you and not to harm you, plans to give you hope and a future' (Jer. 29:11). We look back at the victories he has already won on our behalf. We rejoice in the greatest of those victories, won on a Roman cross nearly 2,000 years ago, and confirmed by a still-empty tomb. We affirm with the apostle Paul in Romans 8:32: 'He who did not spare his own Son, but gave him up for us all – how will he not also, along with him, graciously give us all things?' There were many times in the year that we battled cancer that we reminded one another of this truth: While we don't know exactly what lies ahead or how this will end, we may be confident to proceed forward, emboldened by the reminders of the faithfulness of God in the places we've been. *'Shouts of joy and victory resound in the tents of the righteous.'* These were the things that resounded in our home, even in the context of terminal cancer.

But what resounds in your home? What pulls your family together, and around what does your family rally? What are the constants – the things that you know will take place in your home even when you're away from your family? The recurring theme in Puritan writings about the godly home is that the most excellent and truly vital pursuit for the family, is family worship. This was proposed and defended for several reasons.

First, family worship is the most vital family pursuit because of our knowledge of the nature and character of God. In 1 Corinthians 6:19-20 Paul writes: 'Do you not know that your body is a temple of the Holy Spirit, who is in you, whom you have received from God? You are not your own, you were bought at a price. Therefore honor God with your body.' What we infer from what Paul is telling us is this: Worship of God is due from that which belongs to him. Our belonging to God is based not only on the fact that he created us, but also on the fact that he redeemed us by the blood of his Son when we rebelled against him. If we truly recognize that we belong to him, how can we do anything but worship him? And if we recognize that redeemed individuals belong to him, then we must affirm that the covenant families he ordained belong to him as well and must worship him collectively!

On one level this sounds like a simple expression of duty. You, the individual and covenant family, are God's possession, and whatever belongs to him must worship its owner. Yet Moses, in speaking collectively of God's covenant people, writes in Deuteronomy 7:6: 'For you are a people holy to the LORD your God. The LORD your God has chosen you out of all the peoples on the face of the earth to be his people, *his treasured possession.*' This is what transforms duty into privilege. To be declared 'God's possession' is an expression of ownership. But to be declared 'God's treasured possession' is an expression of such high worth and value that it remains unrivaled by anything that *self*-esteem may proclaim or offer. In this light, the *duty* of worship becomes the *high privilege* of worship! The worth of the individual, and the worth of the covenant family, is not an intrinsic worth. Our worth and value is measured by the worth (or worthiness) of the one we worship.

The New Testament echoes this principle in Ephesians 1:11-14:

> In him we were also chosen, having been predestined according to the plan of him who works out everything in conformity with the purpose of his will, in order that we, who were the first to hope in Christ, might be for the praise of his glory. And you also were included in Christ when you heard the word of truth, the gospel of your salvation. Having believed, you were marked in him with a seal, the promised Holy Spirit, who is a deposit guaranteeing our inheritance until the redemption of those who are God's possession – to the praise of his glory.

The individual and the covenant family are redeemed 'to the praise of his glory' – to his worship! Worship of God is due from all that belongs to him.

Further, our redeeming God is worthy of more praise than we, as individuals and families, could ever give to him. Listen to the words of Ezra and the Levites as they led the returning exiles in worship: 'Stand up and praise the LORD your God, who is from everlasting to everlasting. Blessed be your glorious name, *and may it be exalted above all blessing and praise*' (Neh. 9:5). No matter how great our blessing and praise of God may be, the glory of his name (and all that it represents) will always far exceed the limited glory our worship reflects.

We read in Hebrews 12:28: 'Therefore, since we are receiving a kingdom which cannot be shaken, let us be thankful, and so worship God acceptably with reverence and awe.' Who is receiving a kingdom that cannot be shaken? Not 'I am', but 'we are' – collectively, the family of God and the families belonging to God. Worship of God is due from all that belongs to him. Is there anything in your family's schedule that identifies your collective belonging to him? Anything beyond your attendance together at church? Can you affirm with confidence, 'Every member of my family knows that we belong to Christ, the One who redeemed us?' Be certain that your children and neighbors can readily identify what is truly valuable to your family. They know where you invest your time. They see where you spend your money. And most of all, they see what gets you excited – and what doesn't. If your family is a covenant family, trusting in the promises of the God of the family, then you must recognize that it is not your own, it was bought at a price. And if your family belongs to Christ, then your family must worship Christ together, for worship of God is due from all that belongs to him.

The second reason family worship is the most vital family pursuit is seen in God's purpose for the institution of the family. In his divine providence, God created us as with a longing for relationship. In Genesis 2:18, God said, 'It is not good for the man to be alone. I will make a helper suitable for him.' So he created Eve from the rib of the man and he gave her to him to complete him and to satisfy the need for relationship within him. In an ongoing way, God continues to meet that fundamental need primarily through the family. The psalmist affirms this in Psalm 68:6, 'God sets the lonely in families,' and Psalm 113:9, 'he settles the barren woman in her home as a happy mother of children.'

In the context of this need being satisfied, God also prepares us for eternity. We understand so very little about what our relationships in heaven will be like. We're told in Scripture that there will be no marriage, but we're led to believe that in one way or another our relationships with our children will remain somewhat intact. Consider David's words in 2 Samuel 12. His servants were puzzled that while the child born as a result of his sin with Bathsheba was still living, though obviously sick, he fasted and wept. But when the child died, he got up and ate! David answered (vv. 22-23), 'While the child was still alive, I fasted and wept. I thought, "Who knows? The LORD may be gracious to me and let the child live." But now that he is dead, why should I fast? Can I bring him back again? *I will go to him, but he will not return to me.*' Some assume that David simply expected to go to the grave, but it appears from the text that David expected one day to join his departed son, and therefore poured out his heart in prayer and fasting on his behalf!

Some years ago I attended a conference in England and visited what has become one of my favorite buildings in Europe, Salisbury Cathedral. Construction on that magnificent structure began in 1220. As it was begun, a resolution was adopted: 'Let us build so great a church to the glory of God that those who come after us will think us mad even to have attempted it.' A noble vision! But can you imagine beginning a construction project that would require nearly a century to complete? If you were the bishop of Salisbury who oversaw the hiring of a master builder, do you know what would be one of the fundamental criteria in your selection process? Certainly you would look for a proven craftsman. But you would also look for a man with a son, and a heart to pass on to him his craft and skill. No one builder would live long enough to complete the project. His responsibility was to train his son, and even his grandson, to build well and finish the project.

This is our calling as well. The building of the kingdom of God does not end with us. It extends to our children, and to their children after them. Consequently, the goal that I've repeatedly communicated to my family and church is this: we must invest ourselves toward training and encouraging our children to develop and embrace an even stronger faith than we as their parents today possess. Only in this way will we effectively prepare our children, and their children after them, for eternity.

It is through the family that God intends to equip us for our eternal home. This is affirmed by the scope of the promises of salvation. Consider the recipients of these promises: 'The promise is for you *and your children* and for all who are far off – for all whom the Lord our God will call' (Acts 2:39); 'Believe in the Lord Jesus, and you will be saved – *you and your household*' (Acts 16:31); '(Peter) will bring you a message through which you *and all your household will be saved*' (Acts 11:14). Because of their covenantal design and scope, the promises of salvation are intended not only for individuals, but also for the families they represent.

Our children have been placed in our homes and entrusted to our care to be equipped for heaven! That purpose is specifically identified in Malachi 2:15: 'Has not the LORD made them one? In flesh and spirit they are his. And why one? *Because he was seeking godly offspring.* So guard yourself in your spirit, and do not break faith with the wife of your youth.' Reflecting on this, Samuel Davies wrote:

> The family is the nursery for heaven; yet it cannot be if you banish devotion and worship from it. Can you expect that godliness shall run on in the line of your prosperity if you habitually neglect it in your houses? If you omit this duty you live in direct opposition to the purpose for which the family was created... and your family will become the nursery for hell.[2]

God instituted the family as the nursery for heaven, a place where we and our children after us may be prepared for our eternal home. How, then, can any family effectively equip and prepare its members for the worship that goes on unceasingly in heaven if they are not worshipping together in their homes? Again, Samuel Davies writes:

> Is it as likely that your children will make it their principal business in life to secure the favor of God and prepare for eternity, when they see their parents thoughtless about this important concern, as if they saw you every day devoutly worshipping God with them, and imploring his blessing upon yourselves and your households? Their immortal souls are entrusted to your care, and you must give a solemn account of your trust. If you desire to bring down the blessing of heaven upon your families, if you desire for your children to make their houses the receptacles of religion and convey their faith to the next generation, then begin and continue the worship of God in your families from this day to the close of your lives.[3]

---

[2] Davies, Samuel, 'The Necessity and Excellence of Family Religion,' in *The Godly Family* (Pittsburgh, PA: Soli Deo Gloria Publications, 1993), p. 22.
[3] Ibid., p. 15

How clearly is God's purpose for the institution of the family reflected in your home? Does the way you lead your family in worship express an eager anticipation of being with them in eternity? These are questions that need to be considered each day, for our natural tendency is to become distracted from what is eternally valuable and consumed with what is trivial. The eternal destination of those we love most in this life is at stake.

The third reason family worship is the most vital family pursuit is that the New Testament views the family as a microcosm of the church. In his book, *Quest for Godliness*, J. I. Packer says:

> The Puritans crusaded for a high view of the family, proclaiming it both as the basic unit of society and a little church in itself, with the husband as its pastor and the wife as his assistant, subordinate indeed in the chain of command, but a key figure in the ongoing pastoral process none-the-less.[4]

This perspective was based upon passages like 1 Corinthians 16:19, which the New International Version translates, 'Aquila and Priscilla greet you warmly in the Lord, *and so does the church that meets at their house.*' The Greek text, however, does not include the words, 'that meets at', which would make the most literal translation 'and so does the church in their house.' John Calvin, in his commentary on 1 Corinthians, writes: 'A grand and noble thing it is when the name of "church" is bestowed, as in this passage, on a single family, yet it is desirable and necessary for all godly families to be trained up to be so many little churches. The apostle here is deliberately speaking in commendation of the family of Aquila and Priscilla, on account of its being a kind of small church. Let us learn thus to lead our families, that they may become true churches.' Calvin cites in the same context Romans 16:3 ('Greet Priscilla and Aquila, my fellow workers in Christ Jesus. Greet also the church in their house') and Philemon 1 ('Paul, a prisoner of Christ Jesus, and Timothy our brother, To Philemon our dear friend and fellow worker, and to the church in your home').

From this perspective, we may infer that nearly all of what the New Testament teaches regarding the life, worship, and discipline

---

[4] Packer, J. I., *A Quest for Godliness: The Puritan Vision of the Christian Life* (Wheaton: Crossway Books, 1990), p. 270.

of the church applies as well to the Christian home. What, then, is God's posture toward a Christian family that does not regularly and consistently worship together in their home? The same as his posture toward any local church that fails to engage in corporate worship. Consider the words spoken to the nation of Judah, when they failed to worship: 'Have I been a desert to Israel or a land of great darkness? Why do my people say, "We are free to roam; we will come to you no more"?... My people have forgotten me, days without number. In spite of all this you say, "I am innocent; he is not angry with me." But I will pass judgment on you because you say, "I have not sinned"' (Jer. 2:31-35). The same prophet extends this judgment in family language in Jeremiah 10:25, 'Pour out thy fury upon the heathen that know thee not, and upon the families that call not on thy name' (KJV).

If the Bible views the godly home as a church, then our greatest honor and our highest privilege is realized when our homes are characterized as places of worship. *'Shouts of joy and victory resound in the tents of the righteous.'* What an incredible privilege to celebrate around our tables the One whom angels celebrate unceasingly in heaven! How much like a true church is your home?

Maybe that question would be more honestly answered from another perspective, one to which the Puritans often referred. They recognized that Scripture views the father of a Christian home as the *prophet* and *priest* of that home. We might be more comfortable with the imagery of the *pastor of the home*, but their use of 'prophet' and 'priest' in this context was much more deliberate and precise in what it pictured. In Biblical history, a prophet was the special and unique mouthpiece whom the Lord would use to bring his word, by his authority, to his covenant people. When the prophet delivered God's message, it was usually preceded with the words, 'Thus says the Lord.' The implication was 'Thus says the Lord *to YOU!*' In other words, to reject the words of the prophet was to reject God himself – and stand in peril of judgment as a result. But to accept the prophet's word was to submit to God's authority expressed through those words, and to become a recipient of God's blessing as a result. In similar fashion, the Christian father serves as a prophet in his home. He is called to be God's mouthpiece, proclaiming the Word of God to his family, his household church.

Numerous examples could be cited of fathers in godly homes bringing the word of God to their covenant families.

Think back to Genesis 18:19, where God expresses his purpose in choosing Abraham: 'For I have chosen Abraham, *so that he will direct his children and his household after him to keep the way of the* LORD by doing what is right and just, so that the LORD will bring about for Abraham what he has promised him.'

In Exodus 12:24-28, as Moses records the instructions given to the elders and fathers of Israel concerning the Passover, the clearly stated purpose is to tell the next generation of the work and word of God:

> Obey these instructions as a lasting ordinance for you and your descendants. When you enter the land that the LORD will give you as he promised, observe this ceremony. And when your children ask you, 'What does this ceremony mean to you?' *then tell them,* 'It is the Passover sacrifice to the LORD, who passed over the houses of the Israelites in Egypt and spared our homes when he struck down the Egyptians.'

In these, and in so many other passages, the Christian father is presented as the prophet of his home. He is called to be God's mouthpiece, proclaiming the Word of God to his family, his household church.

The calling of the father doesn't end there. The Puritans also saw that the Christian father is called by God to be a priest in his home, one who faithfully brings God's covenant people (his family) into the very presence of God. When the priest of the home brings his family into the presence of God, he does not bring them as *spectators* to worship, but always as *participants*. That participation in worship begins with the confession of sin, seeking forgiveness. I'm always moved by Job's example in this regard. His seven sons and three daughters would take turns holding feasts in their homes, but after each of these times of feasting, 'Job would send for his children and have them purified. Early in the morning he would sacrifice a burnt offering for each of them, thinking, "Perhaps my children have sinned and cursed God in their hearts." This was Job's regular custom' (Job 1:5). It strikes me that Job didn't simply *worry* about how his children were developing spiritually, nor did he stop at praying *for* them. Instead, as a priest, he assembled them together, and would lead them in offering sacrifices and in confession of sin, seeking forgiveness. Notice that the verse ends with, 'This was Job's regular custom.'

This would be a good place to stop and ask a question. How well have you trained your children to confess their sin and seek forgiveness from, and reconciliation to, the ones from whom their sin separates them? Or better, what kind of example of seeking forgiveness and reconciliation have you set before those in your home? Husbands, when was the last time your wife or children heard you say, 'I was wrong, and I'm sorry. Would you please forgive me?' Conversely, how will the members of your family ever learn to seek forgiveness for their sin if you, the priest of your home, do not model before them the confession and repentance that forgiveness demands? I've found that in raising my children, it is inadequate to lead them to say 'I'm sorry' when they have hurt someone, for that admission focuses on the offender, rather than on the offended party. It isn't the offender, but the offended who has borne the weight and hurt of the offense. Therefore, the offender must focus on the offended and humbly ask for forgiveness. This is where godly reconciliation takes place – not only between our children, but also between their parents.

The second purpose for which the priest of the home brings his family into the presence of God is to teach them the appropriate way of expressing worship and praise to the One who created and sustains their family. Again, we find many examples of this in Scripture, as far back as Adam and Eve and their children.

> Now Abel kept flocks, and Cain worked the soil. In the course of time Cain brought some of the fruits of the soil as an offering to the LORD. But Abel brought fat portions from some of the firstborn of his flock. The LORD looked with favor on Abel and his offering, but on Cain and his offering he did not look with favor. So Cain was very angry, and his face was downcast. Then the LORD said to Cain, 'Why are you angry? Why is your face downcast? *If you do what is right, will you not be accepted?* But *if you do not do what is right*, sin is crouching at your door; it desires to have you, but you must master it' (Gen. 4:2-7).

How was Cain supposed to know what was the right and acceptable way to come to God in worship? The same way Abel had come to know what was right and acceptable: his father, Adam, the prophet and priest of their home, had taught both of his sons how to worship in a manner acceptable to their Creator. Because Adam had modeled that worship and taught that worship, God held Cain responsible for what was required of him.

The third purpose for which the priest of the home brings his family into the presence of God is to take them to the throne of grace, presenting their needs and requests to the one who sits upon that throne. It is there that anxiety gives way to calm, confusion gives way to order, and complexity gives way to simplicity. Our homes must be places of prayer – distinctively so. The Christian father, as a priest, is the one whom God holds accountable to take the initiative in responding to the complexity and crises that confront his family. Yet that initiative, in a godly home, will always direct the attention of that family first to the God who has promised to meet all our needs 'according to his glorious riches in Christ Jesus' (Phil. 4:19).

I find it interesting that at the end of Colossians 3, Paul turns his attention to godly living throughout the relationships within our homes. Then at the end of that progression of thought, he writes: 'Devote yourselves (in the context of families within Christian homes) to prayer, being watchful and thankful' (Col. 4:2). As we've seen thus far, each of us must understand, and submit to, God's design for our respective roles in the family. What brings real cohesion to all these roles, and brings order to all the conflicts, frustrations, and crises that arise within them, is each one's willingness to be devoted to prayer – beginning with the priest of the home.

It's been with great amazement and gratitude that I've watched my children progressively embrace the doctrine of the providence of God. We've taught them to be thankful in prayer, recognizing that every good gift they receive is an expression of God's gracious hand extended to them in love and compassion. In some places, this comes more easily than in others. For example, this past summer our older son played in the Dixie youth AA baseball championship game, and as first-baseman made a significant contribution to their win. My wife's first question to him as we got in the car was,

'Michael, who was ultimately responsible for your ability to play well and to help your team win?' He responded, 'God was, and I've already thanked him!'

But there are other places where acknowledging that same gracious hand of God extended in love and compassion to us is not quite so easy. We saw that as we learned together to pray in a God-honoring way during Amy's illness. During that intense battle with cancer, I began recording some of what God had led us to ask of him. As we approached what would be our last Christmas together, I wrote down what we had begun to pray together as a family:

> O Sovereign Lord, help us today to recognize and affirm,
> That in every detail of our experience, nothing exists or occurs
> Outside the unfolding purpose of your sovereign design,
> And cause us to rest securely in the sure knowledge that every step
>   on this path
> Is lovingly designed to draw us into an ever deepening,
> And ever more intimate, knowledge of you.
> Enable us to see that there is nothing cold, unaffected, or simply
>   methodical
> About your sovereign working in our lives,
> Only the personal, intimate, and warm embrace
> Of the Sovereign Lord drawing us to himself,
> And quietly displaying in us and through us his glory. Amen.

I've been greatly encouraged by the collection of Puritan prayers in Arthur Bennett's book, *The Valley of Vision*. Centuries old, these prayers are yet frequently repeated and firmly embraced both in our church and in our home. I've slightly adapted the words of one of those prayers – one to which I've often anchored my tumultuous thoughts and emotions:

> My Father, you are good when you give, when you take away;
> When the sun shines upon me, when the night gathers over me;
> You have loved me before the foundation of the world,
> And in love did redeem my soul;
> You love me still, in spite of my hard heart, ingratitude, distrust.
> Your goodness has been with me during another year,
> Leading me through a twisted wilderness:

In retreat helping me to advance, when beaten back making sure
    headway.
Your goodness will be with me in the year ahead;
I hoist sail and draw up anchor,
With you as the blessed pilot of my future as of my past.
I bless you that you have veiled my eyes to the waters ahead.
If you have appointed storms of tribulation, you will be with me
    in them.
If I have to pass through tempests of persecution and temptation,
    I shall not drown;
If I am to die, I shall see your face the sooner;
If a painful end is to be my lot, grant me grace that my faith fail
    not;
If I am to be cast aside from the service I love, I can make no
    stipulation;
Only glorify Yourself in me whether in comfort or in trial,
As a chosen vessel always fit for your use. Amen

God extends to us a tremendous offer in his Word. In Hebrews 4:16 we read: 'Let us then approach the throne of grace with confidence, so that we may receive mercy and find grace to help us in our time of need.' The Christian father, as the prophet and priest of his home, recognizes that God's most precious gift to his family is grace. And he recognizes, therefore, that his family's most valuable resource is grace – grace that is offered and extended to his family *that* they may live lives of worship, and grace that is experienced in its fullest expression *as* they live lives of worship.

How much like a true church is your home? How clearly is the message of grace displayed in the roles and relationships within your family? As you may see, the key to answering that question lies in the degree to which the husband and father in that home is faithfully serving as prophet and priest.

But let's make this more practical. What is involved in family worship? It can be as simple as the husband and wife reading a portion of God's Word together and then praying with one another. To this can be added the singing of hymns, psalms, and choruses. With our young children, we do a variety of things. We generally read Scripture, or from a story Bible (Catherine Vos' *A Child's Story Bible* is excellent for children and adults alike). We also memorize scripture passages together. We allow them to select which hymns or songs they wish to sing on a given evening. As our children grow older, we periodically include a chapter or two of different missionary biographies in our time together. We've worked on memorizing the Children's Catechism, and now the Shorter Catechism. In addition, we have often used a number of aids to family worship, such as *A Big Book of Questions and Answers*, written by one of my former seminary professors, Sinclair Ferguson. We talk about our lives, about God's providence, his character, and his faithfulness. And then we pray. Sometimes my wife or I will pray for all of us. Sometimes just the two boys and I will pray. Sometimes Emily and the two girls will pray. Other times we'll assign prayer requests to each member of the family and take a longer time in prayer. Variety seems to keep our children much more engaged and enthusiastic about our time of family worship.

This raises a further question. How often should family worship take place? The Puritans answered this question generally and specifically. Generally, our whole lives are to be expressions of worship! Every part of our daily schedule is an opportunity to lay hold of, and communicate, God's mercy and grace. In Deuteronomy 6:5-9, Moses writes:

> Love the LORD your God with all your heart and with all your soul and with all your strength. These commandments that I give you today are to be upon your hearts. Impress them upon your children. Talk about them when you sit at home, and when you walk along the road, when you lie down and when you get up. Tie them as symbols on your hands and bind them on your foreheads. Write them on the door frames of your houses.

The father in particular (again as a prophet) not only speaks the words of God's truth to his family, but he also models that truth through his practice, and *calls his family to imitate him*. How much of your practice would you want your family to imitate? How many of your attitudes would you want your family to imitate?

Does this sound unreasonable? Listen to God's Word: 'Remember those who led you, Imitate their faith' (Heb. 13:7); 'Be imitators of me, just as I am of Christ' (1 Cor. 11:1); 'The things you have learned and received and heard and seen in me, practice these' (Phil. 4:9). Deuteronomy 6:8 summarizes this so clearly, 'Tie them (these commands) on your hands and bind them on your foreheads.' The standard for our children's thinking, attitudes, and behavior must be illustrated by *your* thinking, attitudes, and behavior! What this simply means is that your entire life is to be an expression and display of worship before your family. Isn't that what Paul is saying in Romans 12:1: 'Therefore, I urge you, brothers, in view of God's mercy, to offer your bodies as living sacrifices, holy and pleasing to God – this is your spiritual act of worship'?

To make certain this is clearly understood, Moses makes practical references to specific, general occasions throughout the day in Deuteronomy 6:7: 'when you sit down' (preparing and enjoying meals, waiting in a Dentist's office, watching a baseball game); 'when you walk along the road' (ten minute errands with your children in the car, carpooling to school, endlessly long road trips while on vacation); 'when you lie down' (putting kids to bed, snuggling on the couch, swinging in the hammock); and 'when you get up' (waking the family, eating breakfast, arranging the schedule for the day, writing the 'to-do' list). Generally, our whole lives are to be expressions of worship and must therefore visibly display worship before our families.

Specifically, the Puritans taught that there should be at least two scheduled times of family worship – morning and evening – that each day would begin and end in worship together. This was based on the biblical pattern seen in Psalm 141:2 ('May my prayer be set before you like incense [the part of Old Testament worship usually offered in the morning], may the lifting up of my hands be like the evening sacrifice') and Psalm 92:2 ('To proclaim your love in the morning, and your faithfulness at night'). They believed that morning was the time to request Divine help and enablement as they reaffirmed their dependence on the God of the covenant who had promised to meet their failure with mercy and their inadequacy with grace. Then, evening worship was an opportunity to collectively express their gratitude to Him for His tender care and gracious providence.

Both morning and evening times of family worship were opportunities for the members of the family to challenge and encourage one another to faithfulness, recognizing the natural tendency for discouragement, bitterness, and the deceitfulness of sin to become a hardening influence in all of their lives. 'But encourage one another daily, as long as it is called Today, so that none of you may be hardened by sin's deceitfulness' (Heb. 3:13). They recognized that encouragement for the Christian comes when we're reminded of the truth – truth that easily becomes obscured not only through the busyness, pressures, and preoccupations of our daily lives, but also through its pleasures and amusements.

The Puritans regarded family worship with vital urgency. They recognized that the family, even then, was a battlefield, one on which a spiritual war was being waged, and in which the souls of its members were the prize. They also recognized that the battle had a conclusion, already determined by God, toward which all history was deliberately moving forward. This intensified their determination to be families that worshipped together, faithfully, reflecting the challenge of Hebrews 10:25, 'Let us encourage one another – *and all the more as you see the Day approaching.*'

Their writings, and the practice to which they led, evidenced a logical progression as to the desired effect of this worship. The practical end of the encouragement that came to the family through their worship together was the practice of obedience to the revealed will of God. That obedience was not simply an outgrowth of the will, it was a result of the pursuit of wisdom and its effect on the mind. But even that wasn't the heart of what the encouragement of family worship produced in the lives of their family members. The central goal from which wisdom and obedience would grow was *passion for Christ*, and its radically life-transforming impact on the affections.

For many, the recurring temptation is to view family worship as a duty, which demands unflinching obedience. But that mentality can produce feelings of guilt. For example, on those mornings when you end up rushing around trying to get everyone where they belong on time, and consequently leave little time for worship before you go your separate ways. But worshipping together as a family isn't an item to check off the list of 'things to do today'. The worship of God, in any context, is a high privilege. It identifies who we are. It is our passion! Thomas Doolittle records nine motives for family worship that give expression to this great passion:

1) The souls that live in your families are precious and immortal souls.

2) These precious and immortal souls in your families are committed to your charge and care.

3) You have but a little time before you for the performance of this trust.

4) The love that you have toward your family should engage you often to pray together with them.

5) Public reformation will only occur through family reformation as godly faith is handed down from one generation to another.

6) If religious duties are not set up in your family that professes faith in Christ, there will be all the more wickedness abounding in it. If God does not have a church in your house, the devil will have a chapel.

7) Your children will be obedient to their authority if you are obedient to yours as you lead them in family prayer.

8) If you make a profession of faith, and do not worship and pray with your family, you have brought hypocrisy to your home.

9) The neglect of calling upon God with your family will bring the curse of God upon them.[5]

Doolittle supports these motives with a perspective that looks toward death and the hidden reality of what lies beyond. I've adapted his words as follows:

'When you are going to pray, look into the unseen world, take a view of departed souls, and seriously think about their state. Think about what those who have already gone into eternity are enjoying or suffering, and from there create arguments to quicken your hearts when dull, to make you diligent when slothful, and to make you lively and fervent in your duty. Oh, how would a believing view of souls in heaven and in hell help you to persevere in prayer!

'Suppose you saw the glorious saints in heaven, and the happiness which they enjoy there, in that they can sin no more, suffer no more, be tempted no more, nor weep nor sorrow any more. All sin is expelled from those glorious souls, all tears are wiped from their eyes; and they now are full of love to God, enjoying the perfect, perpetual, and immediate fulfillment of the greatest expression of what is truly good. Then think, 'This is the

---

[5] *Puritan Sermons, 1659–1689*, Vol. 2 (1674. Reprint, Wheaton, Ill: Richard Owen Roberts Publishers, 1981), p. 248.

state for which I am hoping, looking, longing, and waiting. Now I am going to beg and pray that I may be fitted and prepared for, and hereafter be possessed of joy,' and then pray as one who longs to participate in that joy.

'Then take a view of poor damned souls, and suppose you saw them with your own eyes, rolling in a lake of burning brimstone, full of the fury of the Lord. Suppose you heard their hideous screaming, their bitter wailing ringing in your ears, saying, "Woe and alas that ever we were born! That we've come to this place of torment! Once we had praying time and hearing time, but we did not take advantage of it for our good. If we had, we would certainly not be in this extremity of pain! We did pray, but we played at prayer, and dallied with that God whom now we find and feel to be to us consuming fire. Yet we burn and are not consumed. We were not in good earnest in those prayers, but now we suffer in good earnest, and are damned in good earnest.

' "Will not God pity us? Will not God have mercy on us? We once thought he would; but we flattered and deceived ourselves, and thought things would be fine because we lived in a praying family. But we did not pray as if we were praying to escape such dreadful torments. We often slept in our prayers; but there is no sleeping here, no ease, no resting here!

' "Oh, that God would try us once more! If we only had a month, or two, to be released and sent to a praying life again! If we were only in time again and in the same circumstances again, as once we were, and had the same possibility, even probability, of escaping these restless torments! But this cannot be, this must not be, this will not be! Time is gone, and we cannot pray again! Oh time, how swift was your motion! We wish that this eternity would hasten as fast as time has hastened! When we had lived twenty years, our life was so much nearer expiration; but here we have been a thousand years, and yet as far from an end as the first moment we came into this dreadfully dark and oppressive dungeon. This only adds to our misery, that we are here and must be here forever! Woe be to us that we are here without any hope of recovery or possibility of redemption and deliverance! Even if our pain were extreme, but not eternal, it might have been the better; or if it were eternal, but not extreme, it might be more easily endured. But to feel that it is extreme, and to know it is eternal, makes our misery inexpressible! Can we not die? Can we not dig into our own selves, and take away our own beings? We are cursed! Oh foolish sinners that we were, who prayed with no life in order to escape eternal death. Damnation is a dreadful thing!"

'Then next consider that one of these two places, heaven or hell, you must shortly, very shortly, enter. When you are going to prayer, look behind you, and you shall see death hastening after you, that death is at your heels. Then look forward, and you shall see heaven and hell before you, yourselves standing upon the very brink of time with the next step into an eternity of sorrow or joy. Where you have seen others to be, there you yourselves must be. There you shall rejoice with them or suffer and sorrow with them, eternally.

'Take a brief look forward in time, before you fall down upon your knees. You might see yourselves lying on your sickbed, your friends weeping and fearing you will die. The physicians are puzzled and at a loss, giving you over for the grave, and you gasping for life, breathing out your last breath. Look but a little before you, and you might hear your friends saying, "He is dead, he is dead! He is gone, he is departed!" and then you might see them carrying you out of your bed, and nailing you up in your coffin. You might see your grave being dug, and men hired to carry you on their shoulders from your house to your grave, relatives and neighbors following after to see you lodged in the dust to lie and rot among the dead.

'Then think, before all this can be done unto your body, your soul has taken its flight into eternity, where it is without change and alteration to be with God or devils forever. Take to heart that on that day you will quickly be in heaven or hell. When you die, heaven must be won or lost forever, and everlasting torments escaped or endured forever.'[6]

These are sobering realities. They are inescapable and unavoidable. God will call us to give an account of how we have managed and encouraged worship in our homes, to the end of equipping those in our homes for that great and final day, that eternal worship may follow.

Finally, we're well accustomed to disciplining our children toward academic, social, and athletic growth which prepares them to succeed and excel in this life. Yet I'm increasingly amazed that we're not determined to challenge, encourage, and discipline our

---

[6] Ibid., pp. 248-49.

children with equal and greater urgency toward the spiritual life and growth that prepares them for the eternity to come.

Samuel Davies asks:

> Is it as likely that your children will make it their principal business in life to secure the favor of God and prepare for eternity, when they see their parents thoughtless about this important concern, as if they saw you every day devoutly worshipping God with them, and imploring his blessing upon yourselves and your households? Their immortal souls are entrusted to your care, and you must give a solemn account of your trust. If you desire to bring down the blessing of heaven upon your families, if you desire for your children to make their houses the receptacles of religion and convey their faith to the next generation, then begin and continue the worship of God in your families from this day to the close of your lives.[7]

It is we parents who must own this responsibility, for in our time together, their vision will be lifted to the infinite, eternal, and unchangeable God who loves them, protects them, redeems them, and equips them for their eternal home. Through family worship, our children will learn to treasure their God as they develop a true passion for him. And they will be prepared, well, for eternity.

> 'So we fix our eyes not on what is seen, but on what is unseen. For what is seen is temporary, but what is unseen is eternal' (2 Cor. 4:18).

QUESTIONS FOR FURTHER STUDY AND REFLECTION

1. What aspects of your schedule or routine reflects your family's belonging and allegiance to Christ? (Ps. 118:14-16; 1 Cor. 6:19-20)

2. What aspects of your family's schedule or routine would lead your neighbors to view your family as a 'little church'?

3. The first question in the Shorter Catechism is answered: 'The chief end of man is to glorify God and enjoy him forever.' How is your daily practice preparing your family for the long term: glorifying and enjoying God *forever*? (Isa. 55:1-2; Matt. 6:20; 2 Cor. 4:18)

4. What does Jeremiah 2 teach us about God's determination for us to be faithful in worshipping him as families? (Jer. 2:9, 31-35)

---

[7] Davies, Samuel, 'The Necessity and Excellence of Family Religion,' in *The Godly Family* (Pittsburgh, PA: Soli Deo Gloria Publications, 1993), p. 15.

5. Whose responsibility is it to take the initiative in leading family worship as a prophet and priest? (Josh. 24:15; 1 Tim. 5:8)

6. Are you regularly praying *with* your spouse and children?

7. Are you regularly reading God's Word *with* your spouse and children?

8. Are you teaching the members of your family, by word and example, to repent and seek forgiveness when they sin?

6

THE STRATEGY TOWARD A
GRACE-PORTRAYING FAMILY

As a pastor, one of my fundamental responsibilities is to constantly challenge our congregation, our leadership, and particularly, our ministry staff, toward evangelism. The more specialized each of our staff members and teachers becomes, the more likely each is to focus exclusively on the subject of his or her ministry. In doing so, the mindset of availability becomes secondary, the vision toward pursuing opportunities to present the gospel becomes obscured, and the church becomes an introspective gathering of people intent on meeting their own needs, pursuing their own objectives, and satisfying their own desires.

Yet as the church, we are the very ones to whom Christ has given the great commission: 'Therefore go and make disciples of all nations, baptizing them in the name of the Father and of the Son and of the Holy Spirit, and teaching them to obey everything I have commanded you. And surely I am with you always, to the very end of the age' (Matt. 28:19-20). It is this one who is with us always who challenges us with his mission, and equips us to pursue it. He challenges us to resist the complacency of an introspective existence, and to expend ourselves in proclaiming his message to a dying world: *forgiveness, reconciliation, and righteousness is freely offered to all who will receive it by grace, through faith in Jesus Christ.* By his death and resurrection, he has conquered sin and death, and through our union with him, we are delivered from the life-long slavery of our fear of death (Heb. 2:15). This is the message that prepares us to die well. This is the message that must be proclaimed to a dying world.

From this perspective I've begun challenging our church toward seven action points that are designed to help us overcome our natural tendencies. By way of introduction, let me encourage you to give them consideration as well.

First, commit to praying that God will use you to introduce *one* non-Christian to Christ this year. At first glance, this sounds like a relatively small goal. But there are many in our churches who would have to think back many years to be reminded of the last person they introduced to Christ.

Second, ask God to identify several non-Christians for you to spend time with. This is vitally important, since most Christians tend to gravitate toward spending their discretionary time with others who think and believe just like they do.

Third, invite those whom God identifies into your life. Invite them to your home for a meal or dessert. Invite them to accompany you to those places you most enjoy visiting with your children – the zoo, the pool, the circus, the mall. Invite them to your children's birthday parties. Invite them to be *with* you.

Fourth, seek to earn credibility by inquiring about their interests, longings, dreams, and mostly, their needs. To do this, you'll first need to be willing to set aside your own needs as you express willingness to help them meet theirs.

Fifth, bring them to worship with you. Don't just invite them, but arrange to pick them up – or arrange to have them over for a meal after the worship service.

Sixth, follow up with them after they've accompanied you to worship. Ask them questions: 'Did you make sense of what was taking place? What didn't you understand? Were you left with any unanswered questions? Would you be willing to come again next week?'

Seventh, repeat and continue the process: pray, identify, invite, earn credibility, bring, follow up. God will honor your faithfulness in making yourself available for his use. Those to whom God leads you will examine your life and your family relationships. And they will draw conclusions regarding the genuineness of your faith and the validity of your relationship with Christ.

Do you know what will in all likelihood be one of the greatest influences on the conclusions they draw? Your relationship with your spouse, and your relationship with your children! As you

looking for God in everything. When you are with your family talk about the reality of the invisible, eternal, and unchanging God as always present. Talk about living our lives before his face. Walk through the woods with your family and talk about what God has made, why we treasure these things, and what delight we take in who He's made us to be and what he has provided for us. Teach yourself, teach your children, teach your family to look for the signature of God in everything.

This is what Moses is driving toward in Deuteronomy 6:5-7 when he writes: 'Love the LORD your God with all your heart, with all your soul, and with all your strength. These commandments that I give you today are to be upon your hearts, impress them upon your children, talk about them when you sit at home, talk about them when you walk along the road, talk about them when you lie down and talk about them when you get up.' Learn to look for the imprint of God in everything around you, and teach your children to delight in his handiwork.

Eighth, read with your family. Teach your children to love good books. Few things will have greater lasting impact on the lives of your children than teaching them to love the books where God is proclaimed. They will never know him apart from his Book (singular) and they will never know him well apart from the books that are written about him, or about people who loved and served him faithfully. Since children love to hear their parents read to them, set aside time on the Lord's Day as a regular opportunity to do so. My wife and I have taken this one step further in learning to thoroughly enjoy reading aloud to one another. It takes a while longer to complete a book that way, but it is time well spent. So even if you don't have children in your home, take time to read out loud to each other on the Lord's Day.

Ninth, look for opportunities to exercise hospitality. Invite people over to your home on the Lord's Day. You don't necessarily need to prepare something fancy. Cook a casserole the day before. Have it ready in the refrigerator so when you get up on Sunday morning you're not frantically trying to put things together. I don't run the kitchen in my home, so I know I'm on thin ice here, but I'm inclined to believe that it is possible to prepare a meal that doesn't require excessive labor for any one person on the Lord's

Day. Then look for people to invite to your home who probably can't reciprocate, or whom other families would not naturally be inclined to invite.

Tenth, exercise compassion. Take your kids with you and visit someone who is lonely, someone who is hurting, someone who really would love to see children, someone who would really love to laugh with you. You don't need to look far to find people who would really benefit from that kind of investment of your time.

The list of suggestions for the profitable use of the Lord's Day could go on and on. But the point in all we've examined is simply this: the use of time is an investment, so invest well in the way you spend this one day in seven, in concentrated single-minded pursuit of communion with our eternal Lover. Learn to reflect longingly upon, and anticipate eagerly, the eternal pleasure of God's presence that awaits you. Allow the eyes of your heart to gaze upon the eternal worship that goes on unceasingly in heaven, worship in which your voice will join when you are drawn into the immediacy of Christ's visible presence. Learn to take deep pleasure in the redemptive rest that is yours in Christ.

> If you keep your feet from breaking the Sabbath; and from doing as you please on my holy day; if you call the Sabbath a delight and the LORD's holy day honorable; if you honor it by not going your own way and not doing as you please or speaking idle words, then you will find your joy in the LORD.... I will cause you to ride on the heights of the land and to feast on the inheritance of your Father Jacob. The LORD will guide you always. He will satisfy your needs in a sun-scorched land and will strengthen your frame. You will be like a well-watered garden, like a spring whose waters never fail. The mouth of the LORD has spoken' (Isa. 58:13-14).

QUESTIONS FOR FURTHER STUDY AND REFLECTION

1. Is the way you spend Sunday as a whole best described as a special investment in God's presence, or as personal gratification?

2. To what degree is your passion for Christ and compassion for people evidenced in the way you spend the Lord's Day?

3. Do you believe that you've fulfilled your duty to God in honoring the Lord's Day by spending one or two hours of corporate worship in his presence?

4. To what extent are you faithfully preparing for worship on the Lord's Day by the way you spend Saturday evening?

5. How is grace central to the faithful observance of the Lord's Day?

8

THE REFORMATION
OF THE GODLY HOME
NEHEMIAH 3:1–32

In spite of all our best efforts and strongest desires, sometimes our intentions toward establishing and maintaining a godly family remain unfulfilled. Our eternal perspective and the vision it produces becomes obscured by the pervasive character of materialism, pragmatism, and rationalism in our culture. Our attention becomes distracted, our hearing becomes distorted, our minds grow dull, our hearts become hard, and our passions grow cold. None of this, generally, is deliberate; it just sort of happens. When it does, the most dangerous effect is not immediately visible. The effect is like a long gash, just below the water line of a large ocean vessel. Above the surface everything goes on as if all was well – at least for a time, but eventually, the effects become evident as the vessel sinks.

The 'gashes' in our lives created by the entrance of materialism, pragmatism, and rationalism from the world are not seen immediately. We keep up the facade of 'all is well', yet in reality, the distraction, distortion, dullness, hardness, and coldness that develops within prevents us from looking at our lives from an eternal perspective. The subtle refrain of *memento mori* is effectively concealed from us. We become distracted from treasuring what is infinitely valuable, and grow increasingly unwilling to die daily as we are preparing to die well in the end. This happens not only to individuals, but it happens to families and even to churches.

If this were a sudden shift, it would be easily identified and, consequently, easily addressed and corrected. But it's been said that this kind of shift in focus is rarely a blowout; it is usually a slow leak. This means that the obscuring of our eternal perspective is recognized, usually, only after some time is past, and we find ourselves asking, 'How did I get in this mess?' That's a great question to ask, but only if it leads to asking, 'How do I get back where I belong?' In answer to this question, the book of Nehemiah provides us with a wonderfully encouraging picture of the process of restoring what has become broken and ineffective.

The third chapter of Nehemiah reads somewhat like a subcontractor's list, beginning in the northeast corner of the city and taking a counter clock-wise tour around the city, describing and explaining who repaired which part of the wall and the extent to which those repairs were done by each person. The natural temptation, when coming to a passage such as this, is to look at it and conclude that it reads much like a genealogy. What's the point of this passage being included in God's authoritative word? It's obvious that some commentators who have written about this book have asked that same question, indicating that this is simply a descriptive list of laborers and their individual projects as part of the great and necessary project of restoring the wall around the ancient city of Jerusalem.

But there is so much more to this chapter than is immediately obvious. As the book of Nehemiah deals directly with the reconstruction of ancient walls that had been destroyed by a conquering army, it allows us to draw some applications with regard to the reformation of the family. The broken-down walls of that ancient city may be seen as a sobering picture of the broken down, lukewarm, hardened, and unsatisfying condition of the hearts of God's people. From this perspective, the application doesn't simply stop with the *individual* before God, it extends to the *family* before God as well.

Many are currently praying for reformation and revival in our land, and rightly so, for there is a desperate need for a fresh outpouring of the Spirit of God. But the focus of that reformation is rarely, if ever, restricted to the individual. Reformation and revival, in Scripture and in history, generally have a corporate focus. In 2 Chronicles 7:14 God says, 'If my *people*, who are called by my name, will humble *themselves* and pray and seek my face and turn from *their* wicked ways, then will I hear from heaven and will forgive their sin and will heal *their* land.' All this is to say that the reformation we desperately need in our land must begin in the smallest corporate structure of society: the home. Both in the seeking and the receiving, reformation begins where we live!

As the book of Nehemiah figuratively presents the imagery of God's mercy and grace poured out in revival, we have, by way of application, a picture of God's mercy and grace poured out in reviving the broken-down, lukewarm, hardened, and unsatisfying condition of the hearts of God's people in God's families. This applies not only to the broken-down character of my own heart and its need for restoration, refreshment, and renewal, but also to the greater view of bringing reformation and revival to my family, and to the community in which we live.

Nehemiah 2:20 ends with an emphasis (a recurring theme of the book) on the grace of God: 'The God of heaven will give us success.' Nehemiah is pointing to the centrality of God's grace in the fulfillment of his purpose in the lives of his people as they look to the reconstruction of the walls surrounding that city. At the very beginning of the next chapter, the focus immediately shifts to God's people becoming personally and aggressively involved in the work that God has initiated. The chapter identifies for us, in a somewhat startling fashion, exactly who is responsible for doing the work of rebuilding the walls of that city, and in so doing, it identifies for us who is responsible for pursuing the reformation and revival that we so desperately need.

Notice first of all, that in chapter three there is no mention of any expert wall builder doing any of the work. There is no record of a stone cutter, a mason, a carpenter, a blacksmith, an engineer. No professional builder listed anywhere in this chapter – just ordinary people trusting God to do what God alone can do while faithfully and obediently getting involved. The principle here is that *God loves to use what we feel is unusable, in order to change what we are convinced is unchangeable.* You may have heard it said that God delights to strike a straight blow using a crooked stick. He loves to use people like you and me to accomplish his purpose, in spite of our sense of inadequacy.

While there are no expert builders listed as doing the work of rebuilding the wall around Jerusalem, the chapter does identify who *began* the work. Verse 1 says, 'Eliashib the high priest and his fellow priests went to work and rebuilt the Sheep Gate. They dedicated it and set its doors in place, building as far as the Tower of the Hundred, which they dedicated, and as far as the Tower of Hananel.' The building of the wall did not include any professional builders, but the work began with the spiritual leaders of that community.

Again, the application is unmistakable: revival begins with our spiritual leaders: in the church as well as in the home. By implication, then, each of us has an obligation to pray for the spiritual leaders of our churches and homes. In the church, elders, pastors, and teachers carry the primary responsibility for seeking, communicating, and pursuing the God-given vision of the church in which they serve. Even deacons, who are often (and wrongly) viewed as 'less spiritual' than elders, are responsible for seeking to communicate and pursue the vision that God has established for the church. Pray for them to be faithful in the roles to which God has called them. In the home, the father (or single mother) is charged with the primary responsibility for communicating and pursuing the vision God has graciously established for the family. Pray for the spiritual head of your family, and for the spiritual leaders of your congregation, because the work of seeking revival begins in the home and continues through the leaders of the church.

But it doesn't stop there. We cannot hold our spiritual leaders solely responsible for seeking the revival we so desperately need. The rest of the chapter, 31 verses, provides us with a long list of ordinary people, led by spiritual leaders, who took their roles seriously and trusted God implicitly as they personally got involved in the work that so desperately needed to be completed. Notice where these ordinary people began, for where they began rebuilding the broken down walls is where we must begin in building toward reformation and revival.

It is critical to understand that the life of Jerusalem could not be renewed unless the *entire* wall was rebuilt. That ancient city was built with religious and social and civil structures at the center, and around those structures were the homes and the businesses of its inhabitants. In fact, some of the homes of the people in Jerusalem were built as part of the wall and many were built just opposite the wall on the main thoroughfares just inside the stone walls. Now, if the entire wall was going to be rebuilt, whom would you assign to repair each part of the wall?

The answer, I believe, grows out of a phrase that the writer repeats six times in Nehemiah 3. In verse 10, he says, 'adjoining this, Jedaiah son of Harumaph made repairs *opposite his house.*' In verse 23, 'Beyond them, Benjamin and Hasshub made repairs *in front of their house*; and next to them, Azariah son of Maaseiah, the son of Ananiah, made repairs *beside his house.*' In verse 28, 'Above the Horse Gate, the priests made repairs, *each in front of his own house.*' Again, in verse 29, 'Next to them, Zadok son of Immer made repairs *opposite his house.* Next to him, Shemaiah son Shecaniah, the guard at the East Gate, made repairs.' Then in the last part of verse 30, 'Next to him, Meshullam son of Berekiah made repairs *opposite his living quarters.*'

Now imagine, for a moment, that you live in the ancient city of Jerusalem and you are in bed in your comfortable home. Early one morning, the alarm sounds! The ram's horn! You stumble out of bed and rush to your door. As you open it, your eyes are met with a terrifying sight. The soldiers of your own city are running, fully armed with weapons of battle, through the streets toward the towers to which they are assigned. This can mean only one thing: an invading army has appeared and is preparing to attack the city! You climb the tower near your home and, to your great dismay, find yourself staring at a vast, heavily armed and well-equipped army arrayed on the hill opposite the city. A war is about to begin and the prize is your property, your family, and your life.

What would be going through your mind at his point? I'll give you a hint. Think back to the book of Joshua and the first battle in the conquest of Canaan – the battle of Jericho. The first stage of that battle actually took place forty years prior to the collapse of its massive walls. It was a stage that led the Israelites to such unbelieving rebellion that God condemned everyone twenty years old and older to a lingering and reflective death wandering in a vast wilderness graveyard. The first stage was the sending of spies. Their fundamental responsibility was to determine the status of the enemy – not primarily where they were particularly strong, but where they were particularly *weak*! Ancient near eastern battles were often preceded by sending spies or scouts out to go around the enemy's city to find the weakest, most poorly defended, part of the wall. And at that point of special vulnerability, the attack would begin.

If the weakest part of the wall was near your own home, what would happen to your home and to your family when the battle began? It doesn't take much imagination, does it? The weakest part of the wall is where the invaders would mount their most aggressive attack. In so doing, your home would be among the first to be plundered and burned. Your wife and children would be killed, or worse – they would be captured and taken into slavery. Your life, and the lives of those who meant most to you, would be the first to be destroyed, or they might be the only ones destroyed if the invaders were beaten back after making initial progress.

So back to the earlier question. If it was your home that stood closest to the wall, whom would you want to rebuild that broken section of the wall? If it were my home, I would want to be in charge of the rebuilding of that section, because I would want to make absolutely certain that if ever a scout came to look at that city, it wouldn't be the section of wall opposite my home that they attempted to break through. Our challenge is to seek revival, and pursue the godly reformation of our homes, by leading our families to reflect the truth and character of God. There is no greater incentive than to know that the home and the family that you protect is your own. Revival, for this reason, begins where you live. Let me ask you to consider a few questions as a means of examining how faithfully you've been building the spiritual walls that surround your home and defend your family from the enemy's attack:

1) What kind of appetite for God's Word have you fostered in your own life?

2) What kind of spiritual appetite have you encouraged in your children's lives?

3) What kind of interest in the honor and glory of God do you display by the way that you spend your time, by the way that you spend your money, in the kind of videos that get put into the VCR in your home. Ask yourself the next time you put a video in the player, 'How well am I building the spiritual walls around my home as I watch this movie?'

4) How willingly, wives, have you been living under the spiritual headship of your husband? For as you live under your husband's spiritual headship, you are strengthening the spiritual walls around your home; and as you actively resist or passively manipulate your

husband's spiritual headship, you are weakening the spiritual walls around your home.

5) Husbands, how faithfully have you been loving your wife as Christ loved the church? For in so doing you build and strengthen the spiritual walls that defend your home and provide order, stability, and security for yourself and your family within your home.

6) How recently have you taken spiritual inventory in your own life?

7) How recently have you sat down with your children, with your spouse, to help them take spiritual inventory of where they stand in their relationship with Christ?

8) To what end have you been spending recreational time with your husband/wife, and children?

I recognize that a common response to these questions is, 'You don't know how busy I am! I don't have the kind of time these things would require of me.' Yet it amazes me that even a man as busy as Jonathan Edwards, who ministered tirelessly and wrote prolifically, exemplified these qualities in his relationship with his family, and in particular with his children. Ian Murray writes that he frequently took his daughters with him on horseback journeys away from home. With one of his sons he measured Mount Tom. His children were with him when he planted trees and worked in the yard. It is said that when Edwards' family gathered together in the evenings, he relaxed 'into cheerful and animated conversation,' entering 'truly into the feelings and concerns of his children.'[1]

According to Leland Ryken in his book on the Puritans, *Worldly Saints*, 'The Puritans were particularly concerned about the ability of a bad example to wipe out good instruction. One of them [Benjamin Wadsworth] wrote: "Be sure to set good example before your children.... Other methods of instruction probably will not do much good, if you don't teach them by a godly example. Don't think your children will mind the good rules you give them if you act contrary to those rules yourselves.... If your counsels are good, and your examples evil, your children will be more like to be hurt by the latter, than benefited by the former."'[2]

[1] Murray, Ian, *Jonathan Edwards: A New Biography* (Edinburgh: The Banner of Truth Trust, 1987), p. 186.
[2] Ryken, Leland, *Worldly Saints: The Puritans As They Really Were* (Grand Rapids, MI: Academie Books, 1986), p. 83.

Let me try to illustrate the importance of this issue by looking at Psalm 78, where Asaph makes some piercing comments regarding our families in verses 3-6:

> What we have heard and known, what our fathers have told us, we will not hide them from their children; we will tell the next generation the praiseworthy deeds of the LORD, his power, and the wonders he has done. He decreed statutes for Jacob and established the law in Israel, which he commanded our forefathers to teach their children, so that the next generation would know them, even the children yet to be born, and they in turn would tell their children.

The writer is telling us that reformation and revival, in their truest sense, begin in the home. Here the psalmist takes the emphasis off the personal and individual application of salvation, and says that the design of salvation is as much directed toward your children, and grandchildren to come, as it is toward you! What you do now with your family impacts upon the spiritual health, depth, and strength of your children, your grandchildren, your great-grandchildren and their children after them.

Notice in Psalm 78:7 the result of this shift in focus: 'Then (as a result of doing all these things,) they (your children) would put their trust in God.' The Hebrew literally says, 'then your children would be confident in God.' Your calling as a Christian father or mother is not simply that your children would *know about God*, nor is it simply that your children would *know God*, though that is a good thing. Your calling with regard to your children is that they would *learn to be confident in God* – to trust him wholeheartedly, to rest in him quietly, to treasure him supremely. There is a tremendous difference between knowing God and being confident in him.

One evening, as I put our then five-year-old daughter Katy to bed, a thunderstorm was raging outside. She was rather concerned and asked me about the walls that surrounded her bedroom. She asked specifically whether or not they could hold up against the wind and the thunder – and against the lightning especially! I described to her what those walls were made of: solid bricks held together with a special glue called mortar. I told her that ours was a strong house and she could have great confidence in the walls that surrounded her bedroom. But the Lord gave me a great opportunity to take that one step further as I told her about the protection and strength with which God surrounds her. We are not interested primarily in the walls that surround the bedrooms of our children; we're interested primarily in the walls that surround their very lives, the spiritual walls that we as their parents are responsible to build. Our desire for our children is that they learn to be confident in God.

We are told in educational theory that we should do all we can to raise children who are self-confident. That's great, but it is woefully inadequate. Self-confidence in children becomes an end in itself. The confidence in God that this psalm talks about becomes a means to a greater end, 'that they would not forget his deeds but would keep his commands' (Ps. 78:7). The whole purpose in training our children to be confident in God is that they would learn to be obedient to the word of God.

If you are trying to teach your children to be obedient without at the same time teaching them to be confident in the One who will keep them while they are obedient, you are teaching simple behaviorism, and are short-circuiting God's design for their lives. It is only confidence in God that gives our children the stability, courage, and certainty that God will keep them, carry them, and always honor his promises to them as they are obedient to him – even when the consequences seem like their obedience will work to their detriment. Our children are to be brought up to be confident in God, which happens as we faithfully build the spiritual walls around our homes.

This sounds like a wonderful desire to have for our children. It also sounds like an easily fulfilled or naturally pursued desire of Christian parenting, doesn't it? But it isn't. As a matter of fact, Nehemiah says in 4:14, that there is nothing natural in this pursuit: 'Don't be afraid of them. Remember the Lord, who is great and awesome and *fight for your brothers, for your sons and for your daughters, for your wives, and for your homes.*' Nehemiah says this is a battle, and he calls us to be willing to fight for what is so very valuable to us. It won't come naturally and it won't come easily, but he says to engage in that battle, even when it doesn't seem that there is any evidence of fruit or results in the lives of your children in response to what you've been doing. You and I can't force our children to learn. We can't force our children to grow in spiritual depth and maturity. We can however be faithful in teaching and in modeling truth humbly and consistently. No matter how old our children are, we have an ongoing responsibility to teach confidence in God regardless of whether or not we perceive any evidence of spiritual fruit in their lives.

Some years ago I read a report about a study in Taiwan that described an unusual kind of bamboo – unusual in the way that it grows. The farmer takes small shoots from the mother plant and plants them with about a half inch of that shoot showing. For the next three years the farmer tends that shoot: he fertilizes it, he nurtures it, he cultivates it, he weeds around it, he waters it, and does everything necessary for its growth; but for three years there is absolutely no visible evidence of growth. But the report indicated that there was growth, though not visible. All the growth for those three years is below ground. The three year period of growth is designed to support the growth of that plant in the fourth year. In that fourth year, if the farmer has faithfully nurtured and cultivated that barely visible shoot, the bamboo will grow between 60 and 80 feet in one growing season.

Sometimes the spiritual maturity of our children develops in much the same fashion. So we must always remember that our calling as parents and leaders of our homes is not to change our children. That's the role of the Holy Spirit. He grows them. He causes them to reflect the glory and character of his Son. Our role is to teach them and to nurture them faithfully, modeling before them the testimony of our own confidence in God, regardless of the amount of spiritual growth we perceive in their lives.

We can apply this even more broadly. We as parents cannot teach our children to be confident in God unless we ourselves are first confident in him. If you look at the areas in your life where you've struggled, the places where you are most inclined to fall into temptation, you will find that it is in those areas that you struggle with a confidence in who God is and what he has promised. Even as adults, we will never be able to obey him fully until we first trust him implicitly, and are absolutely confident in who he is and what he has promised. If you try to obey him without a confidence in him, then your obedience is going to be driven primarily by fear and guilt. God never intended for that to be his children's motive in serving him and walking with him.

The process doesn't come naturally, neither in our own spiritual development, nor in the spiritual development of the children in our homes. What comes naturally is steady regression and decline. It's been said that to our forefathers our faith was an experience; to our fathers our faith was an inheritance; to us our faith is a convenience; and to our children, our faith is a nuisance. This will be the natural regression if we are not diligently working toward building the spiritual walls around our homes, encouraging a confidence in God within the lives of our children, and in so doing, preparing them to die well in the end.

A few summers ago, the fathers of several of the other boys on Michael's baseball team and I were commiserating over a heartbreaking loss we had endured on the ballfield. We were so concerned about how poorly our infield had played that we decided to give real priority to baseball practice for the next several weeks. We needed to work hard on tightening up our infield, because if we could get our act together there, we'd definitely start winning again! Several of the dads were members of our church, and two others were members of the local Baptist church. The group suddenly grew silent when I said to them, 'You know, if we were as concerned with the spiritual growth of our boys as we are with their ability to field a ball, we would change this entire community and nation.'

We place such a profound emphasis on our children being good in music, being academically strong, being athletically talented, and developing those talents to whatever degree possible. Yet it is amazing how quickly we step aside from our responsibility to work just as diligently toward encouraging in our children an unshakable confidence in their God, and building around our homes impregnable spiritual walls. I believe that we won't experience true revival and lasting reformation in our churches and nation unless we first pursue such reformation and revival in our homes.

All of this comes back to the vision of reality and the perspective on the future that we've considered throughout these chapters. Earlier I mentioned the practice of Jonathan Edwards with regard to his family. I return again to his writings as an illustration of the vision and perspective that is set forth in these pages. Prior to his twentieth birthday Edwards wrote a series of seventy resolutions by which he ordered his life. He begins with this statement, 'Being sensible that I am unable to do anything without God's help, I do humbly entreat him, by his grace, to enable me to keep these resolutions, so far as they are agreeable to his will, for Christ's sake.'³ Following are just a few of these resolutions, which paint a picture of the way he envisioned his life, and pursued the calling his God had set before him.

Resolution #7: Resolved, Never to do anything, which I should be afraid to do if it were the last hour of my life.

Resolution #9: Resolved, To think much, on all occasions, of my dying, and of the common circumstances which attend death.

Resolution #17: Resolved, That I shall live so, as I shall wish I had done when I come to die.

Resolution #48: Resolved, Constantly, with the utmost niceness and diligence, and the strictest scrutiny, to be looking into the state of my soul, that I may know whether I have truly an interest in Christ or not; that when I come to die, I may not have any negligence respecting this to repent of.

Resolution #50: Resolved, That I will act so, as I think I shall judge would have been best, and most prudent, when I come into the future world.

Resolution #55: Resolved, To endeavour, to my utmost, so to act, as I can think I should do, if I had already seen the happiness of heaven and hell torments.⁴

Sereno Dwight, one of Jonathan Edwards' descendants, comments on these resolutions:

A deep and extensive knowledge of the heart is manifest in these Resolutions, a conviction of its defects, a lively apprehension of its dangers, and an intense concern that all its tendencies should be towards God, and towards everything required by his holy will. There is a remarkable tenderness of conscience discovered in every particular which has been stated. The man who could thus write, was not one who could easily trifle with sin, or who could enter any of its paths without the immediate reproofs of an offended conscience. This man trembled even at the distant view of sin; he

---

³ Edwards, Jonathan, *The Works of Jonathan Edwards* (Edinburgh: The Banner of Truth Trust, 1992), pp. xx.

⁴ Ibid., p. xxi.

could not willingly come near and survey its enticements.... The writer lived as seeing him who is invisible; he set the Lord always before him; encouraging upon all occasions an earnest concern for the glory of God, the grand object for which he desired to live both upon earth and in heaven, an object compared with which all other things seemed in his view but trifles.[5]

Our highest priority must be to display our own confidence in God, toward teaching our children to be confident in our God – to trust him wholeheartedly, to rest in him quietly, and to treasure him supremely as their own God. In so doing, we will effectively build the spiritual walls around our homes. God will change what we are convinced is unchangeable. He will use what we are convinced is unusable. He will use us, but he will call us first to begin at home.

QUESTIONS FOR FURTHER STUDY AND REFLECTION

1. Do the crumbled walls of the ancient city of Jerusalem present a picture of your family and home? In what ways?

2. In what ways do God's grace and our corrective effort need to cooperate to bring spiritual and relational reformation to our families and homes?

3. Whom will God hold accountable to take the initiative toward seeking true reformation in our homes?

4. Can we expect national revival and reformation if we do not first experience it in our homes?

5. Are you willing to be engaged in spiritual battle to secure the spiritual health of those in your homes? (Neh. 4:14)

6. What kind of appetite for God's Word have you encouraged in the lives of those in your home?

7. How zealous are you for the honor and glory of God in your home? What do the movies, music, magazines, etc. that you allow in your home reveal about the answer to that question?

8) Are you raising your children to be confident in their God? (Ps. 78:7)

---

[5] Ibid., p. xxiii.

9

RESPONDING TO TRAGEDY
ISAIAH 28:29

'All this also comes from the LORD Almighty, wonderful in counsel and magnificent in wisdom' (Isa. 28:29).

These are the words to which I directed the attention of my congregation the first Sunday I returned to the pulpit after Amy died of cancer. I began with this passage, and titled my sermon 'Responding to Tragedy,' because many were referring to the death of my first wife and the mother of our four young children in that way – a tragedy. There were also those who were struggling with bitterness, even anger, because God didn't heal her. But the question I felt compelled to address that day was one that would frame our understanding of the very character and providence of God: was Amy's death really a tragedy?

To answer this question we first need to look at how the dictionary defines a tragedy: 'A terrible and unexpected event with disastrous consequences, resulting in profound disappointment and ruin' (my collective paraphrase of several definitions). Is that what happened when the Lord took Amy home? Or is it possible that what the writer of Ecclesiastes says, is true of *this* situation: 'The day of one's death is better than the day of one's birth'?

Further, how can this be viewed as a tragedy when we consider the source of what has taken place? Isaiah writes, '*All* this also comes from the LORD Almighty, wonderful in counsel and magnificent in wisdom.' In the broader context of this chapter, Isaiah was speaking of all the difficult things God was going to bring to bear upon his people. Having listed those calamities, Isaiah writes, 'All this [all these difficult things] comes from the LORD Almighty.'

In the Hebrew, the name 'the LORD Almighty' is really a military title. It is the 'LORD of hosts,' the Divine Warrior, the Captain of the armies of heaven. Isaiah uses this title sixty-two times. Notice that Isaiah does not say that 'all this comes from the Divine Shepherd,' but 'from the Divine Warrior.' Think about this. When you are faced with overwhelming grief and crushing anxiety, when the forces of darkness seem arrayed against you and you don't know where to turn or what to do, whom do you want standing beside you – the Divine Shepherd, or the Divine Warrior who fights our battles for us? They are one and the same, of course, but in my greatest anxiety I want to know that the One who stands with me and holds my hand is the Divine Warrior, the Captain of the armies of heaven. He is the source, the One from whom all this comes. While it is a dark and frowning providence that the Lord has brought to us in Amy's death, it is no less *his* providence. And as William Cowper has written in the hymn, 'God Moves in a Mysterious Way,' *'Behind a frowning providence, he hides a smiling face.'*

But the passage doesn't stop there. You see, normally a powerful warrior is arbitrary in the battles he chooses to fight. If he doesn't stand to gain anything personally from a particular battle, he is not going to be inclined to participate. Not so with our Divine Warrior who fights on our behalf. For the passage goes on to describe him as the One who is 'wonderful in counsel and magnificent in wisdom'.

Let's consider carefully how he is described in this passage. First, he is 'wonderful in counsel'. Normally when we use the word 'counsel' we refer to advice. You seek marriage counsel because you want to avoid or to solve marital conflict. You seek legal counsel because you want advice to know how to interpret and apply the law. But that is not at all what is being referred to here. It isn't God's 'advice' that drives his working, it is his counsel, his eternal, sovereign ruling and overruling purpose and plan, so powerful that he nullifies and frustrates the plans of men while advancing his own. This is what the Psalmist is referring to in Psalm 33:10: 'The LORD foils the plans (the counsel) of the nations, he thwarts the purposes of the peoples, but the counsel of the LORD stands firm forever, the purposes of his heart throughout all generations.' This is God's counsel, his eternal design.

Paul talks about it in Ephesians 1:11:

In him we were also chosen, having been predestined according to the plan of him who works everything according to the counsel of his will.

God has an eternal design by which he moves and drives and works in everything, and the Divine Warrior, the Captain of the armies of Heaven, is driven by this counsel.

Again it is not an arbitrary counsel or plan, for the prophet writes that he is 'wonderful in counsel'. Normally we use the word 'wonderful' as an adjective. We talk about a wonderful dessert, meaning that it was delicious, or a wonderful vacation, meaning that it was enjoyable, or a new outfit that you may have, meaning that it is attractive. But this is not the way it is used in this passage. Here 'wonderful' is a verb. What is deliberately being described is this: the working of God's counsel is so amazing that he leaves us filled with wonder and astonishment, and with deep satisfaction. That's why his counsel is 'wonderful' – it causes us to wonder and stand amazed at what he has done.

I cannot help but think about the way we prayed for Amy during the year she was sick. On August 28, 1995, she was diagnosed with a brain tumor. The news of that diagnosis spread like wildfire. Two days later, after a biopsy, she was diagnosed with a glioblastoma multiforme, the most virulent form of brain cancer. The medical prognosis was set on that day. There are no known survivors of a GBM brain tumor. We thought, 'How wonderful. God has established an absolutely impossible situation, and he has designed to glorify himself by healing her in such a way that no doctor can claim credit.' We prayed, 'God, we plead with you to heal her. We know you are going to do it.' We looked with anticipation to that day when Amy would be healed. But over time our prayers matured and deepened, as we began to pray what Jesus prayed in the Garden of Gethsemane, 'Father, let this cup pass from me. I really wish you would heal her, but more than that – your will, not mine be done.'

Then our prayers began to mature even more, and we began to say, 'Father, don't let us merely be resigned to your will, but teach us to find our deepest and greatest satisfaction in your will.' We prayed that over and over again. I began to hear some of the members in our congregation pray in that way. What a tremendous thing, to ask God not to do what we demand of him, but for him to do what he knows we will ultimately find our deepest satisfaction in. I remember standing at the pulpit of our church on numerous occasions and saying to the congregation, 'I know exactly how God will answer our prayers. God will heal Amy of her cancer – or – he will do something even more excellent.'

The result of all of those prayers is that God, in his infinite wisdom and mercy, for his glory and our good, has determined to pursue that more excellent thing. He has already initiated his design and is even now perfecting it.

If we asked God to do this, and if he answered our prayers exactly as we asked him to answer them, then where is there room for anger? What right does any of us have to be angry in the face of what we have seen God do? There is really only one ground for anger in places of anxiety and uncertainty, and that is unbelief. And unbelief is sin, from which, if you are struggling with such bitterness and anger, you need to repent.

I'm not attempting to make excuses for God or to justify his actions. That's not my role or responsibility. I'm simply attempting to remind you of what you already know is true. Early in this ordeal, one of my college friends told me that you never doubt in the dark what was clear in the light. We don't try to figure out our theology on the basis of the crisis we're experiencing. Rather, we evaluate and respond to our crisis based upon what we already know to be true of our God and his ways.

God is at work, and the outworking of his sovereign counsel is so amazing that he will fill us with wonder and astonishment and deep satisfaction as we observe his hand at work. The only right response to what God is doing in our lives is to look forward with eager anticipation to that more excellent thing which God has initiated and which he has bound himself to complete. 'All this also comes from the LORD Almighty, wonderful in counsel and magnificent in wisdom.'

Do you want to know why this is true? The answer is in that second phrase in the last verse of Isaiah 28. God is not only wonderful in counsel, he is also magnificent in wisdom. The word the prophet uses for wisdom is not the ordinary word you might expect. It is more than the accumulation of knowledge and understanding. Here it is productive, gain-producing, success-affecting, good-resulting wisdom, wisdom that goes way beyond our expectation. It is what Job refers to in a negative way in Job 6:13 where he says, 'Do I have any power to help myself now that success has been driven from me?' That word translated 'success' is the same word which is translated 'wisdom' in Isaiah 28. Job threw up his hands and said, 'I don't have what it takes. I can no longer affect good, I can no longer produce profit or benefit for myself or for my family.'

But God possesses this good-producing wisdom, a wisdom which nothing escapes. The prophet goes on to say that God not only possesses this wisdom, but that he is 'magnificent in wisdom.' Again, the word 'magnificent' is not an adjective, but a verb. It says that God will magnify, intensify, and fully display the glory of his wisdom before our very eyes. It's what the prophet Ezekiel says as he records God's words: 'So I will show my greatness. I will magnify my greatness and my holiness, and I will make myself known, and they will know that I am the LORD' (Ezek. 38:23). God, in his infallible Word, has bound himself to display this wisdom in an incredible way. It is this wisdom which drives this counsel which, as a result, is wonder-producing and awe-inspiring.

This is why God can say in Jeremiah 29:11, 'I know the plans I have for you, plans to prosper you and not to harm you, plans to give you hope and a future.' It is all because the magnificent wisdom that drives his counsel will cause us all to stand in wonder and amazement. 'All this comes from the LORD Almighty, who is wonderful in counsel and magnificent in wisdom.' Did you notice the first word? '*Most* of this comes from the LORD Almighty,' right? No! '*ALL* of this comes from him.'

Back to the earlier question: Was Amy's death really a tragedy? Did this catch God unaware? Will it lead to our ruin? Three times, 'NO!' This is not to say that we did not grieve. The grief was inescapably consuming and, at places, even beyond words. But we were not ruined, we were not crushed, we were not destroyed in the process. 'ALL this comes from the LORD Almighty, who is wonderful in counsel and magnificent in wisdom.'

There was a place where God turned what appeared to be the greatest of all tragedies into the most magnificent triumph ever. It was called 'the place of the skull', where almost 2,000 years ago the disciples of the Lord Jesus stood with their mouths hanging open as they watched their sinless Master, the Man with whom they had spent the last three years, being brutally executed by Roman soldiers. What a tragedy! What an incredible tragedy!

Or was it? What they perceived as a tragedy that day has become our only hope in facing death without fear. Most of us have been exposed to these things all of our lives. We have heard the gospel again and again. We have sung the hymns, we have prayed the prayers, we have recited the creeds, we have heard the stories, we know them well. But some of us have been left unchanged by what we have been exposed to all of our lives, and the familiarity has, I fear, inoculated some against it. If there is a tragedy anywhere, it is here, because that can lead to *eternal* disappointment and ruin.

I leave you with a challenge. When you come to the end of your life, having breathed your last breath, and you open your eyes on the other side, are you convinced that the Lord Jesus will say to you, 'Well done, good and faithful servant. Enter into the joy of your reward'? He's not going to say that to you because you were a person of comparatively high moral standards or because your motives in doing what you did with your life seemed pure. He will welcome you into his eternal kingdom only if you have made what he did on the cross your very own, and if you have allowed that transforming work to pervade your entire life.

Have you embraced for yourself the life-transforming reality of the cross? Have you learned to meditate on the inevitability of your own death, and have you made certain that you truly are in possession of eternal life? Do the choices, words, and affections of your life display a heart and will determined to deal radically with the sin in your life? Are you willing to die daily while you are yet living? Are you faithfully laboring to ensure that those in your family are able to answer these questions as well?

God did for us what we are unable to do for ourselves. He has sought us out in our eternally terminal condition. At the cross, the infinite, eternal, and unchangeable God unleashed the full fury of his wrath against your sin, and mine, which he had placed upon his Son. His eternal Son died a brutal death so that you and I might come to our own death without fear, and say, 'The day of my death will be better than the day of my birth.'

QUESTIONS FOR FURTHER STUDY AND REFLECTION

1. Is there ever a true 'tragedy' in the life of a Christian?

2. How does the statement, 'You do not doubt in the dark what was clear in the light' apply to times of wrestling with crisis?

3. In what ways has God magnified his glory to you as you've learned to trust him – especially in places where you did not understand what he was doing, or why?

10

REFLECTIONS OF A NEW WIFE
AND MOTHER

BY EMILY POTTS HARTMAN

In the fall of 1996, I began a study of the Puritans and how the views of these God-fearing people affected and influenced the godly home. My classroom, however, was not on a campus taught by knowledgeable professors, nor did I learn from researching books and articles on the subject. Instead, God placed me in a home where many of the noble and honorable characteristics of the Puritans were interspersed through the lives of a modern, twentieth-century family. Through unique circumstances, our Sovereign God made me a partner in learning, teaching, and implementing many of the Puritans' values within a very special family, that would later become my own. The pages that follow are a snapshot of God's grace at work in our lives.

One autumn afternoon, I arrived at my apartment, weary from a day's work at a new job, my first 'real' post-college job. After moving from a small town in Mississippi to Boston nearly a year before, I had finally landed what I thought was the perfect job in a small book publishing company. With a great feeling of accomplishment for having succeeded on my own, I was certain that this was the place for me, and was working hard to make sure I was proving myself in this field. When I checked the mail that afternoon, I found a letter addressed to me. By the return address, I assumed it was from my six-year-old friend Katy Hartman and was excited to hear from my favorite little person. Katy, the daughter of my parents' pastor and dear friend, was a sweet, little girl with whom I had developed a close relationship and corresponded over the last year. When I opened the letter, I was surprised to find it not from Katy, but from her dad, Ed.

As I read the carefully chosen words written painfully on the page in my hand, tears streamed down my face. Ed shared how difficult the past few weeks had been for him and his children, Michael (8), Katy (6), Abigail (3), and Daniel (2), since the death of his wife and their mom, Amy. He went on to describe how the Lord had sustained them through this dark valley. I was surprised by his confidence in the Lord's faithfulness and his trust in the Lord's goodness – even in the midst of such heartache. He shared with me his love for my parents, especially my dad as they had become dear friends over the previous year, and thanked me for being Katy's friend. Still wondering why he was writing all this to me, I turned the page. As I continued to read, I realized Ed was asking me if I would consider becoming his children's nanny. The young woman who had been working for him for the last year was leaving and he needed help. He described the responsibilities in detail and said he would adjust whatever was needed in order to make this work for me. Then in closing he wrote:

> Please pray with me about your potential role in all this. I should say that I do have a number of other options – but none is exactly what I feel my kids really need, and frankly, I'm hesitant to entrust them to the care of someone who is less than perfectly suited for them. It's my belief that the lives of my children will have a significant impact on the eternal kingdom of God, and I intend to do all I can to encourage and foster the fulfillment of that expectation. But I need help, and not just anyone will be able to provide what I believe they need. And yet you may. I leave that in God's hands and pray that he will lead you, and us, with unmistakable clarity – for his glory, and for our satisfaction, delight, and good...

At this point my tears were not for them alone, as my compassionate heart became rather self-centered. How in the world could he ask me to leave my life and all I had worked for to be a nanny? There was no way I could do this – or would do it. Though they needed help and my heart went out to them, I was certain that I was not whom they needed at this point. Yet, as I wondered why in the world would he ask me – someone with zero experience, someone he hardly knew, and someone so far from home – my curiosity compelled me to at least spend some time considering his request.

As I mulled over the tremendous decision that lay before me, I felt a persistent tug at the corner of my self-centered heart. Part of it, I'm sure was my wriggling away from the guilt that I knew would be mine if I rejected this sweet family. Also, for some time prior to this, I had been convicted of my rebellious lifestyle and spiritual decline, and it seemed this request was pricking my conscience to seek a different path than the one on which I was headed. But now, as I better understand the work of the Holy Spirit, I am certain that this tug was his working in my heart to make me uncomfortable in the place where I was until I moved to where he wanted me to be. So...

Several weeks later, with tears in my eyes, and much reservation in my heart, I loaded my life into a few suitcases and headed home to Mississippi. My plan was to help the Hartmans out for nine months, while I applied to graduate school. I assumed I could do just about anything for nine months, then I could get on with my life. In addition, I knew enough of the how the Lord works to quote Romans 8:28 and trust that he would use this period in my life to grow me and lead me in a path that was good. But even as I was making that long trek toward home, I was still terribly uncertain about my decision. So many people had told me I was making a huge mistake in leaving my job and the opportunities offered by a big city to be a baby sitter in my home town. Was I? I really didn't know. I just knew I could not tell this family, 'No.'

How grateful I am that God did not show me from the beginning of this new venture where he planned to lead me in the months ahead. I would have certainly run as far and fast as my legs could carry me! But what I did not see from the beginning, God had planned from before the foundation of the world. His plan placed an unqualified, inexperienced, independent, and immature young woman in the perfect situation for a crash course in parenting, patience, love, humility, dependence, repentance, forgiveness, and grace – among other things – to break me, mold me, and make me stronger, while drawing me gently, yet irresistibly back to himself.

This new chapter in my life began immediately. The first several months of my new job were the most challenging, emotional, and exhausting I had ever been through. My responsibilities included keeping house, which I had never done very neatly. I was asked to prepare meals, and I had never before attempted to cook much more than macaroni and cheese from a box. The practical duties of my job were not nearly as challenging as taking care of the four precious children. I had almost no idea how to teach, entertain, discipline, instruct, or even care for the basic needs of any children, much less four who had recently lost their mom.

Every day I left the Hartman house completely exhausted. The longer I was there, the more I realized how incredibly unqualified and inexperienced I was and wondered why in the world God had led me down this path. But at the same time, the Lord gave gifts of encouragement reminding me that though this was difficult and even discouraging, I was exactly where he wanted me to be, surprisingly enough. I was shocked at how much love could flow from four little hearts towards someone they hardly knew. There was something totally refreshing about walking into the house first thing in the morning and being bombarded with hugs and squeals of delight. I can remember Daniel, who was then two-years-old, standing in his baby bed shouting, 'EM-MA-LEE! EM-MA-LEE!' It always made me smile to hear them say my name with such affection and excitement. Abigail often wanted to be cuddled and hugged, holding her little arms up saying, 'Hugga' me,' which of course, I loved doing. Michael and Katy would get so excited to bring good grades home to share with me and to have a new nanny as a play mate. I think what touched me most was that nearly every time I heard them pray, at least one child would thank God for bringing me to be their nanny. I was amazed that though I could not offer them what they needed, could not give them all they wanted, and was not qualified for this position, they embraced me wholeheartedly and loved me just as I was. I loved being loved by them and found gratification in being needed by them. Even though my energy tanks were empty at the end of each day, I left the Hartman home with a full heart.

It wasn't only the affection and appreciation of the children that the Lord used to confirm my being in the right place. I saw something in this family that I wanted for myself. I remember when I was deciding whether or not to move home, my mom wrote me a letter with this advice: 'Emily, just think. You can learn how to raise a family by learning from Ed. You will see how a godly family operates. That way, when you have your own family, you will know so much more. This may be the most valuable experience of your lifetime.' She was exactly right about observing a godly family first hand. I was impressed from the beginning with how well-behaved the kids were, how kind and sweet they were to each other, and how well they responded to Ed. It was fun to watch Ed play with his kids, making them laugh until they hurt, and then when discipline was necessary, I was able to see a loving father show them their sin and lead them to repent and be forgiven. It was encouraging to see Christ as central to this home. This was displayed so clearly as Ed and the children grieved, and yet at the same time were remarkably settled about what God had done and was doing in their lives. This amazed me, until I learned what steps were taken to promote this peace in the children and in Ed. Ed and Amy had taught their children about God's providence in children's vocabulary. The kids had learned to pray for God to heal their mom, or to do something even greater, for his glory and for their good. So when God took their mom and wife home, they believed that beyond their great pain and loss, God had an even better plan for their lives. God's grace in this caused them to worship a good and faithful God rather than become embittered because he did not give them what they so desperately wanted.

These children had a view of eternity than few others could attempt to grasp. Each day the family worshipped together. We sang, 'When I get to Heaven', 'My God is So Big,' and hymns such as 'Like a River Glorious,' 'Blessed Assurance,' 'God that Madest Earth and Heaven,' and 'Amazing Grace.' It was amazing and humbling for me to hear these young children lift their voices in praise to the same God who had taken their mother away from them. What may be even more amazing is at the same time as they were wiping tears from their eyes and bandaging their broken little hearts, they were thanking God for sending me to be their new nanny. It was not long before God placed an inexpressible, undeniable, irreversible love and connection between me and each member of this precious family... even the dad.

My friendship with Ed grew as we became partners, so to speak, in raising his children. He spent hours training me to manage things in his absence. From the beginning, even before I made the decision to move, Ed promised me that he would do all he could to help me succeed at my new role as nanny, and he did. He was a great source of encouragement for me, which was surprising after all he was going through. God was using Ed to point my gaze Godward, giving me a solid foundation on which to build the child-like trust that God was giving to me. I was growing in my relationship with the Lord by leaps and bounds, seeing and understanding many things for the first time. When I accepted the position as nanny, I hoped that I could provide something valuable to this family, but I never imagined that I would be the recipient of so many things of value – eternal value.

What I began to learn was that just as I needed Ed for so much, he, too, needed me. After dinner, we had family worship, put the kids to bed, and then Ed and I talked together. Many of those evenings, Ed would do all of the talking. He would tell me about Amy, describing with a smile and tears how amazing she was. It was obvious to me how much he loved her. He explained to me how the brutality of her illness and death left him debilitated. But at the same time he had a glimmer of hope in his eyes that shone through in the way he spoke of God's goodness to his family during Amy's illness and of his certainty that God would continue to provide abundantly for them as he had in the past. As he often expressed gratitude for my being there for the children and him, I listened quietly with the growing realization that God placed me in this family because we needed each other.

The closeness we experienced in our times together deepened our friendship more than we imagined. Several weeks after my arrival, I began to see some changes in Ed. He was laughing a little more, crying a little less. On occasion, we would spend time together without the children, giving us opportunities to learn about each other. He seemed truly interested in what I thought, which amazed me considering I am twelve years younger than he. We both found ourselves enjoying one another's company and looking forward to our time together.

One day, after an afternoon of shopping for Christmas presents for the kids, Ed treated me to dinner at a nearby restaurant. We were enjoying our time together when suddenly the conversation shifted direction. Leaning over a small table in the corner of the restaurant, Ed shared how much he had enjoyed getting to know me and the time we had spent together. He then proceeded to ask me if, without making any commitment, I would at least be open to the possibility of God's leading us into a relationship that went beyond friendship.

I was shocked! At first, I thought he was out of his mind, as questions, emotions, and confusion swirled in my own mind. As I thought about Ed, his intelligence, his love for the Lord, his sensitive heart, his crystal clear blue eyes that are always honest – even painfully so sometimes, and his love for his children, I knew I admired him, but I wasn't convinced that I would be willing to deepen our friendship any further. Yet as I thought about where our relationship was at that point, I knew that I felt something for him, something I couldn't quite label. It was more than friendship, but fear kept me from calling it anything else. I did know, however, that I missed him when I wasn't with him, and that had to count for something. As I looked into his eyes, knowing he was waiting patiently and anxiously for a reply, I said with a shaky voice and tears of anxiety in my eyes, 'Yes. I would be open to the possibility of something more than friendship, but I want you to know that I have reservations. I've always said I would never marry a man who has been married before; never marry someone with children; never marry a pastor; and I would never, ever move back to this town. So, I don't know what to do with all of that.'

Ed was so calm. He looked at me and said that if the Lord wanted me there, he would overrule my fears and give me a peace that would enable me to receive all of this with open arms. If not, he would close the door, lead me to graduate school, and provide for his family by other means.

But it wasn't other means that the Lord had in mind. As we continued to spend time together trusting the One whose guidance we sought, the Lord knit our hearts together, giving us not just a mutual admiration, but a growing love for each other. He also did what Ed said he would, in diminishing my fears and giving me peace about my place in this family. So, when Ed kneeled before me on a quiet star-lit night and asked me to become his wife, I was thrilled to tell him once again, 'Yes!' What joy filled my heart as I looked at this family that would soon be mine! God was fulfilling his promise to give beauty for ashes, the oil of joy for mourning, the garment of praise for the spirit of heaviness, and we celebrated our marriage as the Hartman family once again became whole.

The commitment I made to Ed on our wedding day was one that included much more than dishes, chores, carpooling, and instructing the kids. I had become an official member of a new family, taking on the role of co-pastor of 'a little church'. This would include learning to pastor children and learning to co-labor with my husband as his wife. I've since adopted our four precious gifts from the Lord, and I'm living a life that would be impossible apart from God's grace. I came into the picture ill-equipped, insecure, unqualified and inexperienced, and God has become the Supplier of all I need to make me a pastor's wife and mother. My mother-in-law has repeated to Ed and me that God will not give more grace until we have embraced the grace He's already given. I have seen this first-hand as our family has faced the challenges of losing a wife and mom and adjusting to a new one; and as I have learned to be a new wife and mom, all at the same time.

Ed's study of the Puritans and the tools they commended toward developing godly marriages and families has provided a secure and stable foundation for our own marriage and family. We're growing to understand the concept of treasuring what is most valuable and making our choices from there, which we are teaching our children, as well. We challenge one another to grow in our relationships with the Lord, as we pray together daily, encourage one another with God's Word, and hold one another accountable as we see sin creeping into our lives. While confronting one another's sin (or being the one confronted) is not pleasant, we have found that it leads to repentance, forgiveness, and restoration which is necessary for a growing relationship with the Lord and with each other. We are learning together our need to be humbly dependant upon the Lord for the ability to love, serve, and honor one another and our need to live lives of ongoing repentance in the face of our continued failure.

God has blessed us with a marriage that is both satisfying and growing in richness. It has not been without conflict or difficult times, but it has been carried by God's grace, as he has provided for us every step of the way. I have found sheer delight in sharing everything with Ed, especially in contrast to my previous desire for independence. With Ed I share my time, my closet, my thoughts, my tears, my laughter, my not-so-funny jokes, my fears, my problems, my joys, my body, my life. The two have become one – what a gift from God that has been!

Becoming an instant mother has also brought unexpected delight. The first time I was called 'Mom' was on our wedding day. As Ed and I were greeting guests at the reception outside at my parents' home on a beautiful May afternoon, I felt a tug on the bottom of my wedding dress. Abigail, who was then four years old, was smiling up at me as she asked if it was okay for her to call me 'Mom' yet. With tears in my eyes and a huge smile on my face, I said, 'Of course.' She giggled and ran away to play with a friend. That was my first introduction to real motherhood. Though I did not hold my children as babies or watch them take their first steps, God had entrusted to me Michael, Katy, Abigail, and Daniel for me to love them and raise them, along with Ed, not just to be healthy, happy, well-rounded children, but to glorify the Lord and enjoy him forever, all in preparation for eternity.

One of my roles as a mother is to teach our children, with Ed, the duty and privilege of worship. Worship was of vital importance to the Puritans, and has become a foundation for richness in our family. I learned a great deal about family worship when I was the nanny, because Ed and Amy had set a pattern of worshipping with the kids daily as a family, which has continued as I have become part of the family. When the kids were younger, we had family worship each evening after supper. But as they've grown older and schedules have become more complex, we now have family worship in the morning around the breakfast table, as we read God's Word, sing hymns, go over our memory verses and Catechism, and pray. Beginning our day here reminds our children, as they head out the door for school, that they are children of the King who must look to him throughout the day in dependance and humility for grace and forgiveness.

Some evenings we read from a children's Bible story book, from which I have probably learned as much as the kids have, or we sometimes read either a Bible question and answer book or a missionary novel. Usually we try to encourage the kids to think reflectively about what we've read, applying it to their young lives. And then, every evening either one of us or all of us lift before God our praise, thanksgiving, concerns, and confessions of the day.

Our children are usually excited about the intimacy with their family and with their God during our family worship time. But they have learned that worship isn't just what we do at church or at home when we are all together for family worship time. Ed and I remind them that worship is something that goes on throughout the day, and must be the purpose of their lives. We've been given countless daily opportunities to point their gaze Godward. We remind the children throughout the day of their need for a Saviour, as we see them struggle with their own sin. We often ask each of the children at dinner time what their favorite thing of the day was and why, as we point them to Jesus. Our greatest goal and challenge is to teach our children to glorify God and enjoy him forever as they progressively learn to live lives of worship.

While we all know at least the foundational aspects of worship, we are selfish, arrogant, and independent people who love to try to handle things on our own and who persistently choose to worship ourselves and the idols we've created rather than our Creator. As I look at who I am in Christ, who he has called me to be as a mom and wife, and what he requires of me in loving Ed faithfully, sacrificing for my family, and in raising my children to know him, love him and walk with him for his glory, I see my desperate need for his abundant grace. Knowing how Christ's righteousness is supposed to change me and even believing it will change me is not enough to transform me from a selfish, prideful, independent woman into a humble, sacrificial, loving wife and mother. I will fail miserably as a wife and mother except by the grace of God, received as I walk in dependence upon him. This is a lesson Ed and I are struggling to learn, and one we are teaching our children, as even they need to see their total dependance upon the Lord. Romans 14:23 says, 'Everything that does not come from faith is sin,' which means I can do all of the right things in raising godly children and being a faithful wife, but if I do them apart from faith, or humble dependence on God, recognizing there is nothing within me that is good or able to please him, I am loving, serving, and sacrificing in sin. My life must be one that is a walk of faith, as Romans 1:17 says, 'The righteous shall live by faith.' I am declared righteous and must now walk in that righteousness as I walk in humble dependence on the Lord. This is absolutely vital in relating to Ed and the children. As hard as I might try, I do not have it in me to be a loving, faithful wife and mother. I must look to the Lord in an ongoing way for grace to make me whom he has called me to be.

All of this leads to the obvious question, 'What happens when we inevitably fail to live up to this standard?' Scripture teaches that repentance is inseparable from faith. God calls us as his children to continually walk by faith look to him for grace. Yet at the same time he knows we will fail; so he also calls us to recognize our sin, confess it, turn to him for a clean heart, and then turn away from our sin. This is repentance, and living a life of ongoing repentance is necessary for growing in our relationship with the Lord, with our spouse, and with our children.

A promise we have made to one another in our family is to keep short accounts, not building up hurt and bitterness towards one another, which means we must forgive quickly and also look carefully at our hearts to see our sin. This requires God's grace, as our natural tendency is to assume we are right and the other surely must be wrong, and it also requires sacrifice, for clinging to that hurt often feels better than offering forgiveness. As parents, it is our responsibility to help our children to see their need to ask for forgiveness when they have offended each other, as well, not just saying, 'Sorry,' with a smug attitude, but with a humble heart acknowledging their sin and asking for forgiveness from one another and from God. It is also our responsibility to ask our children to forgive us when we have sinned against them. I do this more often than I'd like to admit, but I'm sure not often as I should. It is a humbling thing to go before a six-year-old whom I have recently corrected for being unkind to his sister and ask forgiveness for my being impatient and short with him. Yet probably the best tool for teaching them repentance is their seeing true repentance in their parents. Repentance reminds us that we are far more sinful than we even know, and even our righteous acts are filthy rags. We need a Savior, who loves us more than we can imagine, to cleanse us and restore us to himself, that he may also restore us to one another, as husband and wife, parent and child, sister and brother.

'Therefore, in view of God's mercy, present your bodies as living sacrifices, holy and pleasing to God, which is your spiritual act of worship' (Rom. 12:1). As God's treasured possession, I am able to look to him in humble dependence for the grace I need to live a life of sacrifice for my husband and children, and come to him in repentance when I offend him and them, all of which is part of how I am called to worship the One who gave his life for me. It is for this life of worship that God created me. And God made us a family, through unique circumstances, so that we might together learn to worship him. How we carry this out today, prepares us for eternity, as God is even now preparing us for the worship that goes on unceasingly in heaven.

Abigail came home from Sunday School several weeks ago reporting to us that someone in her class said that he didn't like Sundays. Her teacher said, 'If you don't like Sundays, you won't like heaven, because heaven is like one great big worship service.' On one hand she's right. The worship that we participate in on Sundays and throughout our lives is a dim picture of what we will do for all eternity as we sing with the angels, 'Holy, Holy, Holy is the Lord God Almighty who was and is and is to come.' It is our role as parents to teach our children how to worship with his people. We do this on Sundays as we teach them to listen and sing with God's people in church, both by our example in joyfully participating in worship and as we set guidelines for them to follow. In our family, we have encouraged our children, even our youngest, to take notes during church, follow along in the hymn book and in the Bible, and participate in the creeds and Lord's Prayer. We don't let our kids draw in church because I think that teaches them that they are too young to worship. We began bringing Daniel into 'big church' as he calls it, just before he turned three, but only to the evening services which are smaller and more casual. On his third birthday, we made it a privilege and gift for him to worship with us, so he saw it that way. We teach our children that church is not an hour to endure, but it is a celebration where we can worship in God's house with his people, which further prepares us for the worship that we will one day enjoy for all eternity in heaven.

As our children are growing older, they are learning to embrace worship for themselves, treasuring what is eternally valuable. They are being taught to worship a God who not only has given them a house, a nice school, clothes, a family who loves them, food, and lots of toys, but to worship a God who took their first Mommy home to heaven. They understand that they are to pray for God's will be done, because his way is the best way. They understand that when God has promised to take care of them, he will! They are learning to be thankful in all things as part of worshiping God. None of these lessons comes easily; they have learned much as they watched their first mom die. Though this has been difficult for all of them, God has used it to give us the opportunity to teach them to treasure what is eternally valuable.

Our family has been through as dark and painful a valley as one can imagine, yet we have also experienced the overflowing of joy in the morning. We have begun to learn and see with much more clarity than ever before what it is to be held in the tender hands of an awesome God. He has given us a love for one another that surpasses any we dreamed of. And He's given us opportunities to serve him and worship him as a family, shining his light in us before men to the praise and glory of God.

God's promises have not failed – promises to never leave us or forsake us; promises to complete the work He has begun in us; promises to never stop doing good to us; promises to prosper us and not to harm us; and promises to one day carry us home to heaven. Amy saw God fulfill each promise, as she now rejoices in his glorious presence. And we can look back and see how he has kept those promises to us, and look forward to the day we, too, will be with him in heaven. These promises keep our eyes on our Savior and our feet stepping heavenward, so that we may say with confidence, 'Grace has brought us safe this far, and grace will lead us home.'

A SALVE FOR A SICKE MAN,
OR A TREATISE CONTAINING THE NATURE,
DIFFERENCES, AND KINDES OF DEATH;
AS ALSO THE RIGHT MANNER OF DYING WELL
WILLIAM PERKINS,
UNIVERSITY OF CAMBRIDGE, 1616

EDITED AND REWRITTEN
BY EDWARD A. HARTMAN, 1999

WILLIAM PERKINS

A BRIEF BIOGRAPHICAL INTRODUCTION

William Perkins was born at Marston Jabbett in the parish of Bulkington in Warwickshire, England in 1558. He was educated at Christ's College at Cambridge, where at the age of twenty-four he was elected fellow. During his university days he was known as a man given to drunkenness and profanity. On one occasion, while walking along the outskirts of the town, he overheard a woman correcting her disobedient child, saying, 'Hold your tongue, or I will give you to drunken Perkins, yonder.'[1] He later wrote that this so arrested him that the pangs of conscience and shame he felt over becoming the town drunk began the process of conversion in his life, ultimately leading him to commit his life to Christ.

It was in the prison in Cambridge that Perkins began his preaching ministry – not as a prisoner, but as one filled with compassion for those held there. He preached there every Sunday, with such passion and power that soon multitudes flocked to the prison to hear him preach. It was not long before he was chosen to be preacher at St. Andrews church in Cambridge, where he ministered faithfully until his death in 1602.

Both in his preaching and his writing, his most notable characteristic was his ability to analyze and isolate the various components of a complex issue and thereby speak to it with simplicity, yet brilliance. His ability to make practical and plain the difficult, doctrinal, philosophical, and social issues of his day

---

[1] Brook, Benjamin, *The Lives of the Puritans*, Vol. 2 (Morgan: Soli Deo Gloria Publications, 1994), p. 129.

amazed both the educated and uneducated alike. Yet there was an amazing unifying comprehensiveness to his work. His constant effort was to confront all of life and its issues with the question, 'What is the will of God in this?' To do this, much of his writing was presented in the context of casuistry, which is 'the science or art of resolving particular cases of conscience through appeal to higher general principles. It may best be understood as a method of blazing trails through the ethical wilderness that too often separates theory from practice, code from conduct, and religion from morality. All men are casuists. Whenever a decision is made, that decision bears a relation, positively, negatively, or indifferently, to a principle or principles which the conscience holds as authorative.'[2]

Perkins' style of writing and speaking soon became known as 'Practical Divinity', and became immensely popular with the people of his day. In 1589, for example, Perkins began writing a series of 'popular books written in sermon style to promote puritan piety'.[3] His writings were translated into a half-dozen languages, and were among the treasured books carried to the new world by the Pilgrims. 'In short, William Perkins was the most famous and influential spokesman for Calvinism of his day, and his works provide a rewarding thoroughfare into the heart of that attitude, so basic to Anglo-American heritage, which we have come to call Puritan.'[4]

---

[2] Merrill, Thomas F., *William Perkins* (Nieuwkoop: B. De Graaf, 1966), p. x.

[3] Packer, J.I., *A Quest for Godliness: The Puritan Vision of the Christian Life* (Wheaton: Crossway Books, 1990), p. 58.

[4] Merrill, Thomas F., *William Perkins* (Nieuwkoop: B. De Graaf, 1966), p. ix.

to call the Scriptures into controversy, which are truth itself. But we must understand the rationale behind what Solomon affirms, for there are numerous reasons which may be brought to the contrary.

The reasons or objections which may be raised to the contrary may be reduced to six headings. The first is taken from the opinion of wise men, who think that the best thing of all is never to be born, and the next best is to die quickly. If it be the best thing in the world not to be born at all, then the worst thing that can be is to die after a man is born.

Answer: there are two sorts of men: those that live and die in their sins without repentance and those which unreservedly repent and believe in Christ. This sentence may be truly affirmed in respect to the first, of whom we may say as Christ said of Judas, 'It had been good for him that he had never been born' (Matt. 26:24). But the saying applied to the second sort of men is false. For to those that in this life turn to God by repentance, the best thing of all is to be born because their birth is a degree of preparation to happiness. The next best is to die quickly because by death they enter into possession of the same happiness. For this cause, Balaam defined the death of the righteous; and Solomon in this place prefers the day of death over the day of birth, understanding this death as that which is joined with godly life, or the death of the righteous.

The second objection is taken from the testimonies of Scripture. Death is the wages of sin (Rom. 6:23), it is an enemy of Christ (1 Cor. 15:26), and the curse of the law. Hence it seems to follow, that in and by death, men receive their wages and payment for their sins; that the day of death is the doleful day in which the enemy prevails against us; and that he who dies is cursed.

Answer: we must consider death from several perspectives: first as it is by itself in its own nature and secondly, as it is altered and changed by Christ. Death by itself is indeed the wages of sin and enemy of Christ and of all his members; and the curse of the law is the very fires and gates of hell. Yet in the second respect, it is not so, for by the virtue of the death of Christ, it ceases to be a plague or punishment, and of a curse it is made a blessing. It becomes to us a passage or mid-way between this life and eternal life, as it were a new gate or doorway, whereby we pass out of this world and enter into heaven. In this respect, the saying of Solomon is most true: for in the day of birth, men are born and brought forth into the valley of misery, but afterward when they depart, having death altered to them by the death of Christ, they enter into eternal joy and happiness with all the saints of God for ever.

The third objection is taken from the example of most worthy men who have made their prayers against death, as our Savior Christ who prayed in this manner, 'Father, if it be your will, let this cup pass from me, yet not my will but your will be done' (Luke 22:42). David prayed in Psalm 6:4-5: 'Return, O LORD, deliver my soul, save me for your mercies' sake: for in death there is no remembrance of you, in the grave who shall praise you?' Hezekiah wept bitterly when the prophet Isaiah had him set his house in order and told him that he must die (Isa. 38:3). In respect of death, now by the examples of the most worthy men – even by the example of the Son of God himself, it may seem that the day of death is the most terrible and doleful day of all.

Answer: when our Savior Jesus Christ prayed thus to his Father, he was in his agony. He then, as our Redeemer, stood in our place and stead to suffer all things that we should have suffered in our own persons for our sins; therefore he prayed not simply against death, but against the cursed death of the cross, and he feared not death itself, which is the separation of body and soul, but the curse of the law which went with death, namely, the unspeakable wrath and indignation of God. The first death troubled him not, but the first and second joined together did.

Concerning David when he wrote the sixth Psalm, he was not only sick in body, but also perplexed with the greatest temptation of all, in that he wrestled in conscience with the wrath of God, as appears by the words of the text, where he says, 'Lord, rebuke me not in your wrath.' By this we see that he prayed not simply against death, but against death at that instant when he was in that grievous temptation. At other times, he had no such fear of death, as he himself testifies, saying, 'Though I should walk through the valley of the shadow of death, I will fear no evil' (Ps. 23:4). Therefore he prayed against death only as it was joined with the apprehension of God's wrath.

Lastly, Hezekiah prayed against death, not only because he desired to live and do service to God in his kingdom, but for a more special reason. When the prophet brought the message of death, he was without an heir from his own body to succeed him in his kingdom. It may be asked, what warrant did Hezekiah have to pray against death for this cause?

Answer: his warrant was good, for God had made a particular promise to David and his posterity after him, that so long as they feared God and walked in his commandments, they should not want for descendants to sit upon the throne of the kingdom after them (1 Kings 8:25). Hezekiah at the time of the prophet's message remembered what promise God had made and how he for his part had kept the condition thereof, in that he had walked before God with an upright heart, and had done that which was acceptable in his sight. Because of this, he prayed against death, not so much because he feared the danger of it, but because he wanted a child to succeed him on his throne. This prayer God accepted and heard; he added fifteen years unto Hezekiah's days, and two years after gave him Manassah.

The fourth objection is that those who have been reputed to be of the better sort of men often have miserable ends. Some end their days despairing, some raving and blaspheming, and some strangely tormented. It may seem, therefore, that the day of death is the day of greatest woe and misery.

Answer: to this I answer, first of all generally, that we must not judge of the estate of any man before God by outward things, whether they fall in life or death. For, as Solomon expresses in the book of Ecclesiastes, as things come alike to all and the same condition is to the just and wicked, to the good and to the pure, and to the polluted, and to him that sacrifices and to him that sacrifices not, as is the good, so is the sinner; he that swears, as he that fears an oath. Secondly, I answer the particulars alleged on this manner. First of all, touching despair, it is true that not only wicked and ungodly persons despair in death, but also repentant sinners, who often in their sickness, testify of themselves that being alive and lying in their beds they feel themselves as it were to be in hell, apprehending the very pangs and torments thereof. I doubt not for all this, but that the child of God who is most dear unto him, may through the gulf of desperation attain to everlasting happiness. This appears by the manner of God's dealing in the matter of our salvation. All the works of God are done in and by their contraries. In the creation, all things were made, not of something, but of nothing, clean and contrary to the course of nature. In the work of redemption, God gives life, not by life, but by death, and if we rightly consider Christ upon the cross, we shall see our paradise out of paradise in the middle of hell, for out of his own cursed death he brings us life and eternal happiness. Likewise, in effectual calling, when it pleases God to convert and turn a man unto him, he does it by the means of the gospel preached, which in reason should drive all men from God. It is as contrary to the nature of man as fire to water, and light to darkness, yet for all this, though it is against the disposition and heart of man, it prevails with him and turns him to God. Furthermore, when God will send his own servants to heaven, he sends them a contrary way, even by the gates of hell, and when it is his pleasure to make men depend on his favor and providence, he makes them feel his anger, and to be nothing in themselves, that they may wholly depend upon him, and be whatever they are in him.

This point being well considered, it is obvious that the child of God may pass to heaven by the very gates of hell. The love of God is like a sea, into which when a man is called, he neither feels the bottom nor sees bank. I conclude, therefore, that despair at the time of death, whether it arise of weakness of nature or of conscience of sin, cannot prejudice the salvation of them that are effectually called. As for other strange events that sometimes occur at the time of death, they are most likely the effects of diseases. Ravings and blasphemies arise out of the disease of melancholy, and frenzies often happen at the end of burning fevers – the writhing of the lips, the turning of the neck, the buckling of the joints and the whole body, cramping and convulsions, which follow after extended illness. Whereas some in sickness have such strength that three or four men cannot hold them down without bonds, it comes not of witchcraft as people commonly think, but of choler in the veins [is physiologically caused]. Though some, when dead, become as black as pitch, this does not argue some extraordinary judgment of God. These and similar diseases with their symptoms and strange effects, though they finally deprive man of his health and of the right of the parts of his body, they cannot deprive his soul of eternal life. All sins prompted by violent diseases and proceeding from repentant sinners, are sins of infirmity, for which, if they know them and come again to the use of reason, they will further repent;

if not, they are pardoned and buried in the death of Christ. We ought not to judge on the basis of this when we know the goodness of his life, for we must judge a man not by his death, but by his life.

If it is true that strange diseases and strange behaviors in death may befall the best man there is, we must learn to reform our thinking of such conclusions at the point of death. The common opinion is that if a man dies quietly and goes away like a lamb (which in some diseases a man may do), then he goes straight to heaven; but if the violence of the disease stirs up impatience and causes frantic behaviors, then men sometimes say that this is a judgment of God, serving to either discover a hypocrite or to plague a wicked man. The truth is otherwise. For indeed a man may die like a lamb and yet go to hell; and one dying in exceeding torment and strange behaviors of the body may go to heaven. By the outward condition of any man, either in life or death, we are not to judge or so state before God.

The fifth objection is that when a man is most near death and is assaulted by Satan, the most dangerous and troublesome is his care, and, therefore, it may seem that the day of death is the worst day of all.

Answer: the condition of God's children in death is two-fold. Some are not tempted, as Simeon, who when he had seen Christ, broke forth and said, 'Lord, now let you your servant depart in peace,' therefore signifying no doubt, that he should end his days in peace. As for them which are tempted, though their case be very troublesome and perplexed, their salvation is not further off because of the violence and extremity of temptation. God is present by the unspeakable comfort of his Spirit, and when we are most weak, he is most strong in us because his manner is to show his power in weakness. For this reason, even in the time of death, the devil receives the greatest loss as he looks for the fiercest victory.

The sixth objection is that violent and sudden death is a grievous curse. Of all evils which befall man in this life, none is so terrible; therefore it may seem, that the day of sudden death is most miserable.

Answer: It is true indeed, that sudden death is a curse and a grievous judgment of God, and therefore not without cause feared of men in the world. Yet all things considered, we ought more to be afraid of an impatient and evil life than of sudden death. Though it be evil, as death as felt in his own nature is, we must not think it to be simply evil, because it is not evil to all men, nor in all respects evil. I say it is not evil to all men, considering that no kind of death is evil or a curse to them that are in Christ, who are freed from the whole curse of the Law. Therefore, the Holy Ghost says in Revelation 14:13, 'Blessed are they that are in the Lord, for they rest from their labors.' This indicates that they which depart this life, being members of Christ, enter into everlasting happiness, regardless of what kind of death they die, even though it may be sudden death. Again, I say that sudden death is not evil in all respects. It is not evil because it is sudden, but because it commonly takes men unprepared and by that means makes the day of death a black day, as if it were a very speedy downfall to the gulf of hell. Otherwise, if a man be ready and prepared to die, sudden death is in effect no death, but a quick and speedy entrance to eternal life.

With these objections answered, it appears to be an obvious truth when Solomon says that the day of death is better indeed than the day of birth. Now I come to the third point: the reasons and respects that make the day of death to compare to the day of a man's birth. All these reasons and respects may all be reduced to this one. The birthday is an entrance into all woe and misery, whereas the day of death joined with God and reformed life is an entrance or degree to eternal life.

Eternal life has three degrees. One is in this life, when a man can truly say that he lives not, but that Christ lives in him. This is the experience of all who repent and believe and are saved and sanctified and have peace of conscience with other gifts of God's Spirit which are the earnest of their salvation. The second degree is in the end of this life, when the body goes to the earth, and the soul is carried by the angels into heaven. The third is in the end of the world at the last judgment, when the body and soul are reunited and enter into eternal happiness in heaven.

Of these three degrees, death itself joined with the fear of God is the second, which also contains in it two worthy steps to life. The first is a freedom from all miseries which have their end in death. Though men in this life are subject to numerous dangers by sea and land and to various aches, pains, and diseases, when death comes, there is an end of all. Again, so long as men live in this world, whatever they may be, in some part they lie in bondage under original corruption and the remnants thereof, including the doubting of God's providence, unbelief, pride of heart, ignorance, ambition, envy, hatred, lust and such sins, which bring forth fruits unto death. To be in subjection to sin in this manner is a misery of all miseries. Therefore Paul, when he was tempted to sin by his corruption, calls the very temptation the buffets of Satan, as though it were a prick or thorn wounding his flesh and paining him at the very heart. Again, in another place, wearied with his own corruption, Paul complains that he is sold under sin, and he cries out in Romans 7:24: 'O miserable man that I am, who shall deliver me from this body of death?' David says in Psalm 119:136 that his 'eyes gushed out with rivers of tears when other men sinned against God'. How much more, then, was he grieved for the sins by which he himself was overtaken in this life? Indeed, it is a very hell for a man that has but a spark of grace to be exercised, turmoiled, and tempted with the inborn corruption and rebellion of his own heart. If a man attempted to devise a torment for those who fear God and desire to walk in newness of life, he could not devise a greater one than this. For this reason, blessed is the day of death which brings with it a freedom from all sin whatsoever. When we die, the corruption of nature is abolished, and sanctification is accomplished.

Lastly, it is a great misery that the people of God are constrained in this world to live and converse in the company of the wicked, as sheep are mingled with goats which strike them, annoy their pasture, and muddy their water. For this reason, David cries out in Psalm 120:5, 'Woe is me that I remain in Mesech, and dwell in the tents of Kedar!' When Elijah saw that Ahab and Jezebel had planted idolatry in Israel and that they sought his life also, he went apart into the wilderness and desired to die. This misery also ends in the day of death, as if the hand of God sorts and singles out those that are his servants from all the ungodly men in this most wretched world.

Further, this exceeding benefit comes by death, that it does not only abolish the miseries, which presently are upon us, but also prevents those which are to come. 'The righteous,' says the prophet in Isaiah 57:1, 'perish and no man considers in his heart;

and merciful men are taken away, and no man understands that the righteous are taken away from the evil to come.' The Lord says in 2 Kings 22:19-20: 'Because your heart did melt, and you have humbled your self before the LORD, when you heard what I spoke against this place ... behold therefore I will gather you to your fathers, and you shall be put in your grave in peace, and your eyes shall not see all the evil which I will bring upon this place.' Paul says in 1 Corinthians 11:32, that among the Corinthians some were asleep, that is, dead, so they might not be condemned with the world.

The first benefit that comes by death and the first step to life is freedom from misery. The second benefit is that death gives an entrance to the soul that it may come into the presence of the everlasting God, of Christ, and of all the angels and saints in heaven. The worthiness of this benefit makes the death of the righteous to be no death, but rather a blessing to be wished of all men. The consideration of this made Paul say in Philippians 1:23, 'I desire to be dissolved.' What, then, is the cause of this desire? That follows in Paul's next words, that by this dissolution he might 'come to be with Christ'. When the Queen of Sheba saw all Solomon's wisdom, the house that he had built, the meat of his table, the sitting of his servants, and the order of his ministers and their apparel, she said in 1 Kings 10: 'Happy are your men, happy are these your servants, which stand ever before you and hear your wisdom.' Much more may we say that they are ten thousand fold happy which stand not in the presence of an earthly king, but before the King of Kings, the Lord of heaven and earth, and at his right hand enjoy pleasures for evermore.

Moses has been renowned in all ages because God afforded him the privilege of seeing his hind parts at his request. What then will be the happiness of seeing the glory and majesty of God face to face, to have eternal fellowship with God our Father, Christ our Redeemer, and the Holy Ghost our Comforter, and to live with the blessed saints and angels in heaven for ever?

In this respect death is clearly seen as being more excellent than life. It may be here that the unsatisfied mind of man will yet further reply and say that even though in death the souls of men enter into heaven, their bodies, though kept tenderly for food, drink, and apparel and having slept many a night in beds of down while living, must now lie in dark and loathsome graves, and there be wasted and consumed by worms. All this is true indeed, but all is nothing, if we will consider rightly our graves, as we should. We must not judge graves, as they appear to the bodily eyes, but we must look upon them by the eye of faith. We must consider graves as they are altered and changed by the death and burial of Christ, who having vanquished death upon the cross, pursued him (death) afterward to his own den, and foiled him there and deprived him of his power. By this means Christ in his own death has buried our death, and by the virtue of his burial, it is as if sweet incense has sweetened and perfumed our graves and made the often decaying and loathsome cabins to become princely palaces and beds of moss, sweet and happy – far more excellent than beds of down. Though the body rot in the grave and be eaten of worms, or of fishes in the sea, or burnt to ashes, that will not be unto us a matter of discomfort, if we consider well the ground of all graces, namely, our conjunction with Christ. While it is spiritual, it is a most real conjunction. We must not imagine that our souls alone are joined to the body or soul of Christ, but the whole person of man, in body and soul, is joined and united to the whole Christ. When we are once joined to Christ in this mortal life by the bond of the Spirit, we shall remain and continue eternally joined with him, and this union once truly made shall never be dissolved. Thus it follows, that although the body be severed from the soul in death, neither body or soul are severed from Christ. The very body rotting in the grave, drowned in the sea, burned to ashes, abides still united to him and is as truly a member of Christ then, as before.

This point we must remember as the foundation of all our comfort and hold it for ever as a truth. Look what the condition of Christ was in death; the same is the condition of all his members. The condition of Christ was this: though his body and soul were severed each from the other, as far as heaven and the grave, neither of them was severed from the Godhead; instead, both did in death subsist in his person. Therefore, though our bodies and souls be pulled asunder by natural or violent death, neither of them, not even the body itself, shall be severed and disjoined from Christ.

It will be alleged that if the body were then united to Christ, it should live and be quickened in the grave, but this is not so. When a man's arm or leg is taken with the dead palsy, it receives little or no heat, life, sense, or motion from the body, yet notwithstanding it remains still a member of the body, because the flesh and the bone of it remains joined to the flesh and the bone of the bodies. Even so may the body remain a member of Christ, though for some space of time it receives neither sense, nor motion, nor life from the soul, or from the Spirit of God.

Furthermore, we must remember that by the virtue of this conjunction, the dead body, though it is rotted, burned, devoured, or howsoever consumed, will, at the day of judgment, rise to eternal glory. In the winter season, trees remain without fruit or leaves, and being beaten with wind and weather, appear to the eye as if they were rotten trees. When the spring time comes again, they bring forth, as before, buds and blossoms, leaves and fruit. The reason is because the body, grains and arms of trees, are all joined to the root, where the sap lies in the winter season, and by this connection the sap is derived to all parts of the tree in the spring time. Even so, the bodies of men have their winter also, in which they are turned to dust and so remain for the space of many thousand years; yet in the day of judgment, by means of their mystical connection with Christ, shall divine and quickening virtue stream to all the bodies of the elect to cause them to live again, to life eternal.

Some will say that the wicked also shall live again.

Answer: they do so indeed; but not by the same cause, for they rise by the power of Christ as he is a judge to condemn them. The godly rise again by the virtue of Christ's resurrection, of which they are partakers by means of that blessed and indissoluble connection which they have with Christ. The bodies of the elect, though they decay and are consumed ever so much in the grave, are still in the favor of God and in the covenant of grace to which, because they have right and title even being dead, they shall not remain so forever, and shall rise to glory at the last judgment. For this reason, the rotting of the body is insignificant in this respect, and the death of the body is no death. Death in the Old and New Testament is viewed as a sleep and the grave as a bed. In it a man may rest, not at all troubled with dreams or fantasies, and from which he shall rise no longer subject to weakness or sickness. He shall presently be translated to eternal glory. The death of the righteous, on this basis, is a second degree to everlasting happiness.

Considering, then, that our connection with Christ is the foundation of all our joy and comfort in life and death, we are in the fear of God to learn one lesson: while we have time in this world, we must labor to be united to Christ, that we may be bone of his bone, and flesh of his flesh. So that we may be assured that we are certainly joined to Christ, we must show ourselves to be members of his mystical body by the daily fruits of righteousness and true repentance. Being once certainly assured in conscience of our being in Christ, let death come when it will, and let it cruelly part both body and soul, as they both remain in the covenant and by this will be reunited and taken up to life eternal.

On the other hand, if men are out of the covenant and die outside of Christ, their souls go to hell. Their bodies rot for a time in the grave, but afterwards they rise to endless damnation. This is why I say again and again, labor that your conscience may testify, by the Holy Ghost, that you are living stones in the temple of God and branches bearing fruit in the true vine. Then you will feel by experience that the pangs of death will be a further degree of happiness than ever you found in your lives, even when you are gasping and panting for breath.

In Solomon's preference of the day of death to the day of birth, he leads us to understand that there is a direct and certain way whereby a man may die well. If it had been otherwise, he could not have said that the day of death is better. In affirming this, he shows that there is an infallible way whereby a man may make a blessed end. Therefore let us come to search out this way, the knowledge and understanding of which must not be reached from the writings of men, but from the Word of God, who has the power of life and death in his own hand.

For a man to die well, God's Word requires two things: a preparation before death and a right behavior and disposition of death.

Preparation before death
The preparation before death is an action of a repentant sinner, whereby he makes himself fit and ready to die. It is a necessary duty to which we are bound by God's commandment. There are numerous places in Scripture which strictly enjoin us to watch and

pray, and to make ourselves ready every day against the second coming of Christ to judgment. The same places also bind us to make a preparation against death, at which time God comes to bring judgment to us particularly. Again, look as death leaves a man; so shall the last judgment find him, and so shall he abide eternally. There may be changes and conversions from evil to good in this life, but after death there is no change at all. Therefore, a preparation for death can in no ways be omitted by him who desires to make a happy and blessed end.

This preparation is twofold: general and particular. General preparation is that whereby a man prepares himself to die through the whole course of his life, a necessary duty which must in no ways be omitted. The reasons are as follows.

First of all, death, which is certain, is most of all uncertain. I say it is certain because no man can avoid death. Further, it is uncertain in three ways. First, in regard of time, no man knows when he shall die. Secondly, in regard of place, no man knows where he shall die, whether in his bed or in the field, whether by sea or by land. Thirdly, in respect of the kind of death, no man knows whether he shall die of a lingering or sudden death, of a violent or natural death. Hence it follows that men should every day prepare themselves for death. Indeed, if we could know when, where, and how we should die, the case would be otherwise, but seeing we know none of these, it stands in hand to look about us.

A second reason serving further to persuade us is that the most dangerous thing of all in this world is to neglect all preparation. To make this point more evident, I will make this comparison. A certain man was pursued by a unicorn. In his flight he falls into a dungeon, and in his fall takes hold and hangs by the arm of a tree. As he hangs there looking downward, he sees two worms gnawing at the root of the tree, and as he looks upward, he sees a hive of most sweet honey, where he climbs up into it, sits, and eats. While he is sitting there, the two worms gnaw in pieces the roots of the tree, until finally the tree and the man all fall to the bottom of the dungeon. The unicorn is death, and the man that flees is every living man. The pit over which he hangs is hell. The arm of the tree is life itself, and the two worms are day and night, the continuance of which is the length of a man's life. The hive of honey is the pleasures and profits and honors of this world, to which men wholly give themselves, not considering their ends, until the tree root, that is, this temporal life, is cut off. Once this is cut, they plunge themselves into the gulf of hell. By this we see that there is good cause that men should not defer their preparation till the time of sickness, but rather every day make themselves ready against the day of death.

Some will say, it shall suffice if I prepare my self to pray when I begin to be sick.

Answer: these men greatly deceive themselves, for that time is most unfit to begin a preparation, because all the senses and powers of the body are occupied about the pains and troubles of the disease. The sick party is exercised partly in conference with the physician, partly with the minister about his soul's health and matters of conscience, and partly with friends that come to visit. Therefore, there must be some preparations made before, in the time of health, when the whole man with all the powers of body and soul are at liberty.

Again, there are some others which imagine and say that a man may repent when he wills, even in the time of death, and that such repentance is sufficient.

Answer: what they say is false, for it is not in the power of man to repent when he himself wills but when *God* wills he may. It is not in him that wills or runs, but in God that has mercy. Christ says that many shall seek to enter into heaven, and shall not be able. Why is this so? Because they seek when it is too late, when the time of grace is past. It is exceedingly foolish for men so much as once to dream that they may have repentance on demand. It is a just judgment that those who condemned God in their life should be condemned by God in their death, and those that forget God in their health should be forgotten by God in their sickness.

This late repentance is seldom true repentance. It is sick and deficient like the party himself, commonly languishing and dying together with him. Repentance should be voluntary (as all obedience to God ought to be), but repentance taken up in sickness is usually constrained and compelled by the fear of hell and other judgments of God. For crosses, afflictions and sickness will cause the greatest hypocrite that ever was to stoop and buckle under the hand of God and pretend faith and repentance and every grace of God, as though he had them as fully as any of the true servants of God. Such repentance is generally counterfeit. In true and sound repentance, men must forsake their sins. But in this, the sin forsakes the man, who leaves all his evil ways only because he is constrained to leave the world. It is a great thing to wish that men would repent and prepare themselves to die in the time of health before the day of death or sickness.

Lastly, it is alleged that one of the thieves repented upon the cross.

Answer: the thief was called after the eleventh hour at the point of the twelfth, when he was dying. His conversion was altogether miraculous and extraordinary, with special reason why Christ called him. While he was suffering he might show forth the virtue of his passion, that all which saw the one might also acknowledge the other. It is not good, therefore, for men to make an ordinary principle of an extraordinary example.

Having seen that a general preparation must be made, let us now examine the duties which must be practiced in the course of our lives to make that preparation.

Meditation
The first is the meditation of death in the time of life. The life of a Christian should be nothing but a meditation of death. A notable example of this is seen in the practice of Joseph of Arimathea, who made his tomb in his lifetime in the midst of his garden. He did this, no doubt, to put himself in mind of death while in the midst of his delights and pleasures. Heathen philosophers that never knew Christ had many excellent meditations of death, though not comfortable in regard to life everlasting. We, that have known and believed in Christ, must go beyond them at this point, considering with things that they never thought of, namely, the cause of death, our sin; the remedy thereof, the cursed death of Christ – cursed, in regard to the kind of death and punishment laid upon him, but blessed in regard to the benefit it provides us. Also, we must consider the imminence of death, which we do when by God's grace we make an account of every present day, as if it were the very day of our death, and reckon with ourselves when we go to bed as though we should never rise again, and when we rise as though we should never lie down again.

This meditation of death is of special use and brings forth many fruits in the life of man.

First of all, it serves to humble us under the hand of God. An example is Abraham, who said in Genesis 18:27, 'Behold I have begun to speak to my Lord, and I am but dust and ashes.' Notice that the consideration of his mortality made him to abase and cast down himself in the sight of God. If we could reckon of every day as of the last day, it would pull down our peacock's feathers, and make us with Job to abhor ourselves in dust and ashes.

Secondly, this meditation is a means to further repentance. When Jonah came to Nineveh and cried: 'Yet forty days, and Nineveh shall be destroyed!' the whole city repented in sackcloth and ashes (Jonah 3:3-5). When Elijah came to Ahab and told him that the dogs should eat Jezebel by the wall of Jezreel and told him also of Ahab's flock that died in the city, it made him to humble himself. The Lord says to Elijah, 'See you how Ahab is humbled before me?' (1 Kings 21:29). Now if the remembrance of death was of such force in one who was a hypocrite, how excellent a means of grace will it be in those that repent?

Thirdly, this meditation serves to stir up contentment in every estate and condition of life that will come to us. Righteous Job in the very middle of his afflictions, comforts himself with this consideration, 'Naked came I forth of my mother's womb, and naked shall I return' (Job 1:21), and again when he says, 'Blessed be the name of the Lord.' Surely as we often meditate on the fact that a man of all his abundance can carry nothing with him in death but either a coffin or a winding sheet, it should force us to turn aside from the insatiable desire for riches and the love of this world. Thus we see what an effectual means this meditation is to increase and further the grace of God in the hearts of men.

In commending this first duty to your Christian consideration and practice, two things must be performed.

First, labor to pluck out of your hearts a wicked and erroneous imagination, by which every man naturally blesses himself and thinks highly of himself. Though he has one foot in the grave, he persuades himself that he shall not die yet. There is no man, because of the corruption of his heart, too old to think that he shall live one year longer. Cruel and unmerciful death makes covenant with no man, yet the prophet says in Isaiah 28:15 that the wicked man makes 'a covenant with death'. How can this be? There is no agreement made indeed, but only in the wicked imagination of man, who falsely thinks that death will not come near him, though wishes it to be destroyed. See an example in the parable of the rich man, who having stored up abundance of wealth for many years, said to his own soul in Luke 12:19, 'Soul, you have much goods laid up for many years, live at ease, eat, drink, and be merry,' but his soul was taken away that very night. Recognizing that this natural corruption is in every man's heart, we must daily fight against it and labor by all might that it take no place in us for so long that it prevails. If it does, we will be completely unfit to make any preparation for death. We ought rather to endeavor to attain to the mind and meditation of Saint Jerome, who testifies of himself on this manner, 'Whether I wake or sleep, or whatsoever I do, me thinks I hear the sound of the trumpet, Rise you dead, and come to judgment.'

The second thing which we are to practice so we may seriously meditate on death, is to make prayer unto God that we might be enabled to resolve ourselves of death continually. David prayed in Psalm 39:4: 'LORD, make me to know mine end, and the measure of my days, let me know how long I have time.' Moses prayed in Psalm 90:12: 'Lord, teach me to number my days, that I may apply mine heart unto wisdom.' It may be asked what men need to pray to God that they might be able to number their days. Can they not determine the number of days with their measurements of the globe of the earth, the spheres of heaven, and the quantities of the stars, with their longitudes, latitudes, altitudes, motions, and distances from the earth? No indeed! By a general speculation we think something of our ends, yet unless the Spirit of God be our schoolmaster to teach us our duty, we will never be able soundly to resolve ourselves of the presence and speediness of death. Therefore, let us pray with David and Moses that God would enlighten our minds with knowledge and fill our hearts with his grace, so we might rightly consider death and live every day and hour as if it were the day and hour of death.

Weaken death's strength

The second duty in this general preparation is that every man must daily endeavor to take away the power and strength from his own death. I pray you mark this point. The Philistines saw that Samson was of great strength, and they attempted to know in what part of the body it lay. When they found it to be in the hair of his head, they wouldn't rest until it was cut off. In like manner the time will come when we must do hand to hand battle with cruel death. It is best, that now, while we have time to search where the strength of death lies, we must with speed cut off his (death's) locks, and relieve him of his power, disarm him and make him altogether useless to prevail against us. Now to find out this matter, we need not to use the counsel of any Delilah, for we have the Word of God which teaches us plainly where the strength of death lies. As Paul says in 1 Corinthians 15:56, 'The sting of death is sin.'

Knowing with certainty that the power and force of every man's particular death lies in his own sins, we must spend our time and study in using good means so our sins may be removed and pardoned. We must daily involve ourselves in the practice of two duties: first, to humble ourselves for all our sins past, partly confessing them again to ourselves, partly in prayer crying to heaven for the pardon of them; second, to come unto God, and to carry a purpose, resolution, and endeavor in all things to reform both heart and life according to God's Word. These are the very principal duties, by which the strength of death is much abated. This mighty and bloody enemy of death is made friendly and tractable, that we may with comfort encounter with him and even prevail. If a man were to deal with a mighty dragon serpent hand-to-hand, he must either kill or be killed. The best thing would be to relieve the dragon of his sting, or of that part of his body where poison lies. Death itself is a serpent, dragon, or scorpion, and sin is the sting or poison with which he wounds and kills us. Therefore, without any more delay, see that you pull out his sting, by the practice of the duties previously mentioned.

Have you been a person ignorant of God's will, a neglecter of his Word and worship, a blasphemer of his name, breaker of his Sabbath, disobedient to parents and magistrates, a murderer, a fornicator, a railer, slanderer, a covetous person? Reform your sins and all others; pull them out by the roots from your heart, and call them off. As many sins that are in you, so many stings of death are also in you to wound your soul to eternal death. Let not one sin remain for which you have not humbled yourself and repented seriously. When death hurts any man, it takes the weapons from the hands of the man. It cannot do us the least hurt but by the force our own sins. Therefore I say again and again, lay this point to your hearts, and spend your strength, life, and health, that before you die, you may abolish the strength of death. A man may put a serpent in his bosom, when he controls the stinger. Likewise, we may let death creep into our body, grip us with his legs, and stab us at the heart, so long as he brings not his venom and poison with him.

Because the former duties are so necessary, as none can be more, I will use some reasons to further enforce them. Whatever a man would do when he is dying, the same he ought to do every day while he is living. Even the most notorious and wicked person that ever was, when he is dying, will pray and desire others to pray for him. He will promise amendment of life, promising that if he might live he would become a practitioner in all the good duties of faith, repentance, and reformation of life. Again, the saying is true, that he who lives as though he is dead must die to his sins while he is alive. Do you wish to live eternally? Then go to heaven for your pardon, and see that now in your lifetime you die to your own sins. Wicked Balaam wanted to die the death of the righteous, but he would by no means live the life of the righteous, for his continual purpose and meaning was to follow his old covetous ways. The life of a righteous man must be in the humbling of himself for his sins and in a careful reformation of life to come. Would you then die the death of the righteous? Look unto it, that your life be the life of the righteous. If you desire to live the life of the unrighteous, you must expect to die the death of the unrighteous. Remember this, and do not be content simply to hear the word, but be doers of it, for you have truly learned no more than what you have actually put in practice.

Enter into eternal life
The third duty in our general preparation to die is to enter into the first degree of eternal life while remaining in this life. As I have said, there are three degrees of life everlasting, and the first of them is in this present life. He who wants to live in eternal happiness forever must begin in this world to rise out of the grave of his own sins, in which by his nature he lies buried, and live in newness of life, as it is said in Revelation 20:6: 'he that will escape the second death must be made partaker of the first resurrection.' Paul tells

the Colossians that they were delivered from the power of darkness in this life and translated into the kingdom of Christ (Col. 1:13). Christ says to the Church of the Jews, 'The kingdom of heaven is among you.' This first degree of everlasting life is when a man can say with Paul, 'I live not, but Christ lives in me' (Gal. 2:20). I find partly by the testimony of my sanctified conscience, and partly by experience, that Christ my Redeemer by his Spirit guides and governs my thoughts, will, affections, and all the powers of body and soul according to the blessed direction of his holy will.

Now in order to say this, we must have three gifts and graces of God, in which especially this first degree of life consists. The first is saving knowledge, where we do truly resolve ourselves that God the Father of Christ is our Father, Christ his Son is our Redeemer, and the Holy Ghost is our Comforter. This knowledge is one part of eternal life, as is indicated by the words of Christ in John 17:3: 'This is life eternal (that is, the beginning and entrance into life eternal) to know you the only God, and Jesus Christ, whom you have sent.'

The second grace is peace of conscience which passes all understanding (Phil. 4:7). Paul says in Romans 14:17 that the kingdom of heaven is 'righteousness, peace of conscience, and joy in the Holy Ghost'. The horror of a guilty conscience is the beginning of death and destruction. Therefore, peace of conscience derived from the death of Christ is life and happiness.

The third is the regiment or life of the Spirit, whereby the heart and life of man is ordered according to the Word of God. For Paul says in Romans 8:14 that 'they that are the children of God are led by the Spirit of Christ'.

Seeing that if we seek to live eternally we must begin to live that blessed and eternal life before we die, here we must be careful to correct two common errors. The first is that a man enters into eternal life when he dies, and not before, which is a flat untruth. Our Savior Christ said to Zaccheus, 'This day is salvation come to your house' (Luke 19:9). This leads us to understand that a man begins to be saved when God effectually calls him by the ministry of his gospel. Whoever seeks to be saved when he is dying or dead must begin to be saved while he is now living. He that would come to salvation *after* this life must begin salvation *in* this life. 'Verily, verily,' says Christ, 'he that hears my word and believes him that sent me has eternal life' (John 5:24) – he who believes in this present life.

The second error is that however a man lives, if when he is dying he can lift up his eyes and say, 'Lord, have mercy upon me,' he is certainly saved. This is a very dangerous and foolish conceit that deceives many. It is as if a thief should reason with himself and say, 'I will spend my days in robbing and stealing, I fear neither arrest nor execution. At the very time when I am to be hung, if I simply call upon the judge, I know I shall have my pardon.' This is a most dangerous and desperate course for a man. The very same is the practice of careless men in the matter of their salvation. For a man may die with the words, 'Lord, have mercy,' in his mouth, yet perish eternally, for 'not everyone that says, Lord, Lord, shall enter into heaven: but he that does the will of the father which is in heaven' (Matt. 7:21).

Die little by little
The fourth duty is to exercise ourselves toward and become accustomed to dying little by little while we live on earth before we die. As men who intend to run a race exercise themselves to running that they may get the victory, so should we begin to die now while we are living, that we might die well in the end.

Some may say, how should this be done?

Answer: Paul gives us direction in his own example, when he says in 1 Corinthians 15:31: 'By the rejoicing which I have in Christ, I die daily.' He died daily, not only because he was often in danger of death because of his calling, but also because in all his dangers and troubles he prepared himself for dangers and troubles. He prepared himself to die. When men make right use of their afflictions, whether in body or mind, or both, and endeavor with all their might to bear them patiently, humbling themselves as under the correction of God, then they begin to die well. To do this is to take an excellent course. He that would die to his greatest sins must begin to do it with small sins. When they are addressed and corrected, a man shall be able to more easily overcome his master sins. In the same way, he that would be able to bear the cross of all crosses, even death itself, must first of all learn to bear small crosses, as sickness in body, troubles in mind, loss of goods and friends, and loss of a good name. These we may appropriately term 'little deaths' and the beginning of death itself.

We must first of all acquaint ourselves with these little deaths before we can be able to bear the great death well. The afflictions and calamities of this life are the harbingers and pursuers of death. We are first to learn how to entertain these messengers, that when death or the Lord himself shall come, we may better entertain him. Bilney the martyr considered this point well, who before he was burned, often put his finger into the flame of the candle, not only to test his ability in suffering, but also to arm and strengthen himself against greater torments in death. You see the fourth duty, which you must by all means learn and remember. We cannot be able to bear the pangs of death well, unless we be first well schooled and nurtured by the many trials we shall face in this life.

Do good

The fifth and last duty is set down by Solomon in Ecclesiastes 9:10: 'All that your hand shall find to do, do it with all your power. For there is neither work, nor invention, nor knowledge, nor wisdom in the grave whither you go.' To the same purpose Paul says in Galatians 6:10: 'Do good to all men while you have time.' If a man is able to do any good service either to God's church, or to the common-wealth, or to any private man, let him do it with all speed and with all might, lest death itself prevent him. He that takes care to spend his days in this way will with much comfort and peace of conscience end his life.

Particular preparation in time of sickness

Now we direct our attention from general preparation to particular preparation, which is in the time of sickness. Here, first of all, I will show what is the doctrine of the Papists (the designation for those who taught the teaching and authority of the Roman Catholic church), and then afterward the truth. By the Popish order and practice, when a man is about to die, he is commanded to do three things: first, to make sacramental confession, especially if it be in any mortal sin; second, to receive the Eucharist; and third, to require his anointing, that is, the sacrament (as they call it) of extreme unction.

Sacramental confession is a rehearsal or numbering of all a man's sins to a priest, that he may receive absolution. Against this kind of confession numerous objections may be raised. First of all, it has no warrant either by commandment or example in the whole Word of God. The Papists say that it does, and they endeavor to prove it in the following manner. He which lies in any mortal sin is by God's law bound to do penance and to seek reconciliation with God. The means of this penance and reconciliation is the confession of all our sins to a priest. Christ has appointed priests to be judges upon earth, with such measure of authority that no man falling after baptism can without their sentence and determination be reconciled. The priests cannot rightly judge, unless they know all a man's sins; therefore all that fall after baptism are bound by God's Word to open all their sins to a priest.

Answer: on one level they are correct when they say that priests are judges, having power to examine and take knowledge of men's sins, and jurisdiction whereby they can properly absolve and pardon or retain them. God's Word has given to man a ministry of reconciliation (2 Cor. 5:18), whereby in the name of God, and according to his Word, he preaches, declares and pronounces that God pardons or does not pardon his sins. This pardon, however, may truly be pronounced and right judgment of the estate of any man without a rehearsal of his sins before a priest. He whose heart soundly and truly repents of one sin will (and must) repent of them all.

Secondly, this confession is overturned by the practice of the prophets and apostles, who not only absolved particular persons but also whole churches without a detailed, verbal confession. When Nathan the prophet had rebuked David for his two great and horrible crimes, David, touched with remorse, said in 2 Samuel 12:13, 'I have sinned,' and Nathan, without further examination, declared to him in the name of God that his sins were forgiven.

Thirdly, it cannot be proved by any good and sufficient proof that this confession was used in the church of God until after five or six hundred years were expired. The confession in use then was either public before the church or the opening of a public fault to some private person in secret. To urge sick men into it lying at the point of death is to lay more burdens on them than ever

God appointed. Those who make it a necessary thing to receive the Eucharist in the time of sickness toward death, and require this to be done privately by the sick party alone, have no warrant for their practice and opinion. There is no danger in the absence of the sacrament, but in its contempt. The very contempt of the Sacrament itself is a sin which may be pardoned, if we repent.

There is no reason why we should think that a sick man is deprived of the benefits and comfort of the Lord's Supper which he received at some point prior to his sickness. The fruit and efficiency of the sacrament once received is not to be restrained to the time of receiving, but it extends itself to the whole time of man's life afterward. Again, the Lord's Supper is no private action, but merely ecclesiastical. Therefore, it is to be celebrated in the meeting and assemblies of God's people, as our Savior Christ prescribes, when Paul says, 'Do this ... when you come together.'

The objection is raised that the Israelites ate the Paschal Lamb in their houses when they were in Egypt.

Answer: the Israelites had then no liberty to make any public meeting for that purpose, and God commanded that the Paschal Lamb should be eaten in all the houses of the Israelites at one and the same instant. This, in effect, was as much as if it had been public.

Again, they claim the canon of the Council of Nicea, which decrees that men being about to die must receive the Eucharist and not be deprived of the provision of food necessary for their journey.

Answer: the Council made no decree touching the administration of the Sacrament to all those who die, but to such only as fell away from the faith in perfection or fell into any other notorious crime and were excommunicated, remaining there until death, and either then or somewhat before repented for their offenses. The canon was made so such persons might be assured that they were again received into the church, and by this means depart with more comfort.

It is objected also that in the primitive church part of the Eucharist was carried by a lad to Serapion, an aged man, lying sick in his bed.

Answer: it was indeed the custom of the ancient church from the very beginning, that the elements of bread and wine should be sent by some of the deacons to the sick, which were absent from the assembly. Nevertheless, here is no basis for private communion. The Eucharist was only sent when the rest of the church openly communed. Those who were absent only by reason of sickness, and desired to be partakers of that blessed communion, were to be treated as if they were present.

Lastly, it is objected that it was the manner of men and women in former times to carry part of the sacrament home to their houses, and to reserve it until the time of necessity, such as the time of sickness.

Answer: the reservation of the sacrament was a superstitious practice, though it was ancient. Outside of its distribution (that is, before it begins, and after it is ended), the sacrament ceases to be a sacrament, and the elements to be elements. As for the practice of those that used to cram the Eucharist into the mouth of them that were deceased, it is not only superstitious, but also absurd.

Another practice was anointing of the body, especially the organs or instruments of the senses. This practice was so the party may obtain the remission of his sins, comfort against all temptation of the devil in the house of death, and strength to more easily bear the pangs of sickness and the pangs of death. The party would then be restored to his bodily health, if it were expedient for the salvation of his soul. This is but an imagination of the mind of man and has nothing to justify it. Appeal is commonly made to James 5 for this purpose. The anointing mentioned there is not of the same kind as this great sacrament of the Papists. First, the anointing of the body described in James 5 was used as a ceremony by the apostles and others when they put into practice this miraculous gift of healing (which is now ceased). Secondly, the anointing of the prophets has with it a promise that the party should recover his health, but the Pope's anointing has no such promise. For the most part the person thus anointed dies afterward without recovery; whereas those who were anointed in the primitive church always recovered. Thirdly, the ancient anointing served only for the procuring of health, but this tends further to the obtaining of remission of sins and strength in temptation.

Having seen the doctrine of the Papists, I come now to speak of the true and right manner of making particular preparation before death. This contains three sorts of duties: concerning God, concerning man's own self, and concerning our neighbor.

Duties concerning God

The first, concerning God, is to seek to be reconciled unto him in Christ, though we have been long assured of his favor. All other duties are secondary, and are of little or no effect without this. This reconciliation must be sought for and is obtained by a renewing of our former faith and repentance in the following manner. As soon as a man shall feel any manner of sickness to seize his body, he must consider its origin within himself, and after serious consideration he shall find that it comes not by chance or fortune, but by the special providence of God. This done, he must go one step further and consider for why the Lord should afflict his body with any sickness or disease. He shall find by God's Word, that sickness comes ordinarily and usually of sin. Lamentations 3:39 says, 'Why should any living man complain when punished for his sins?' It is true indeed that there are other causes of sickness besides sin, and though they are not known to us they are known to the Lord. Even Christ, when he saw a certain blind man and was asked what was the cause of the blindness, answered in John 9:3, 'Neither has this man sinned, nor his parents, but that the works of God should be showed on him.' We, who are to follow the revealed will of God, must make this use of the sickness sent to us for our sins. When Christ healed the man sick with palsy, he said in Matthew 9:2, 'Be of good comfort, your sins are forgiven you'; and when he had healed the man by the pool of Bethesda, that had been sick thirty-eight years, he told him to sin no more, lest a worse thing should happen to him. In both instances Christ leads the men to understand that their sickness came by reason of their sins. So also should every sick man resolve himself.

Once we have laid our finger upon the right and proper cause of our sickness, three things concerning our sins must be performed of us in sickness. First, we must make a new examination of our hearts and lives, and say as the Israelites said in affliction, 'Let us search and try our ways, and turn again unto the LORD' (Lam. 3:40). Secondly, we must make a new confession to God of our new and particular sins, as God sends new corrections and chastisements. In Psalm 32:4 when David had the hand of God very heavy upon him for his sins, so as his very bones were consumed within him, he confessed them unto God, obtained his pardon, and was healed. The third thing we must do concerning our sins is pray more earnestly than ever before, with sighs and groans of the Spirit for pardon of the same sins, and for reconciliation with God in Christ.

In the exercise of these three duties stands the renovation of our faith and repentance, whereby they are increased, quickened, and revived. The more sickness prevails and takes place in the body, the more should we be careful to put them in use, that spiritual life might increase as temporal life is decayed. When King Hezekiah lay sick, as he thought upon his death-bed, he wept for his sins as for other causes, and with all he prayed God to cast them behind his back. David made certain psalms when he was sick, or at the least upon the occasion of his sickness (Pss. 6, 32, 38, and 39). All are psalms of repentance, in which we may see how he renewed his faith and repentance, heartily bewailing his sins, and entreating the Lord for the pardon of them. Manassah, one who fell from God and gave himself to many horrible sins, when he was taken captive and imprisoned in Babylon, prayed to the Lord his God, humbled himself greatly before the God of his fathers, and prayed to him. God heard and answered his prayer, and brought him again into Jerusalem into his kingdom. Manassah then knew that the Lord was God (2 Chron. 33:12-13). What Manassah did in his tribulation is what we must do in the time of our bodily sickness.

Here I have occasion to mention a notorious fault that is very common in this age, even among those that have been in the church all their lives. Men today are so far from daily renewing their faith and repentance, that when they lie sick and are drawing toward death, they must be catechized in the doctrine of faith and repentance, as if they had been recently received into the church. Whoever has occasion to visit the gravely ill shall find this to be true. What a shame is this! A man has spent his life and days in the church for the space of twenty, thirty, or forty years, and at the very end of all, and not before, he begins to inquire into what faith and repentance is and how his soul might be saved. This one sin confirms the great security of this age and the great contempt of God and his Word. Let all men be warned to take heed of this exceedingly great negligence in matters of salvation, and use all good means beforehand, so that they may be able in sickness and in the time of death to put in practice the spiritual exercises of invocation and repentance.

If the sick person cannot renew his own faith and repentance by himself, he must seek the help of others. When the man who was sick with palsy could not go to Christ himself, he got others to bear him in his bed (Mark 2:4). When the multitude prevented them from coming near they uncovered the roof of the house, and let the bed down before Christ. In the same way, when sick men cannot by themselves do the good duties to which they are bound, they must borrow help from their fellow members, who are to help them partly by their counsel, and partly by their prayers to present them to God, bringing them into his presence.

In terms of the help these fellow members are to provide, various duties are to be performed. Saint James sets down four: two concern the sick patient and two address the helpers.

The first duty of the sick man is to send for help. Two circumstances must be considered: who must be sent for and when they must be sent. For the first, Saint James says in James 5:14, 'Is any sick among you? Let him call for the elders of the church.' This refers to not only apostles and all ministers of the gospel, but also to others (as I take it) who were older men, filled and motivated by the Spirit of understanding and prayer, and possessing the gift of working miracles and of healing the sick. In the early Church this gift was for a time so plentifully bestowed on them that believed in Christ, that soldiers cast out devils, and parents wrought miracles on their children. Hence we may learn that though it is principally the duty of the ministers of the Word to visit and comfort the sick, it is not their duty alone, for it belongs to them also which have knowledge of God's Word and the gift of prayer. 'Exhort one another while it is called today' (Heb. 3:13). Again, in 1 Thessalonians 5:11 and 14, Paul says, 'Admonish them that are disordered, and comfort these that are weak.' By all means it should be the duty of every Christian to comfort his brother in sickness.

We must take knowledge of the common fault of men and women when they come to visit their neighbors and friends. They cannot speak a word of instruction and comfort, but spend the time in silence, gazing and looking on, or in uttering words too little or of no eternal purpose. They say to the sick party that they are very sorry to see him in that shape, that they would have him to be of good comfort, but cannot tell by what means. They tell him that they are certain that he shall recover his health and live with them still, and be merry as in former time. Then they say they will pray for him. All their prayers amount to little more than the Apostles Creed, the ten commandments, or the Lord's prayer uttered without understanding. This is the common comfort that sick men get at the hands of their neighbors when they come to them, and all this comes either because they live in ignorance of God's Word, or because they falsely think that the whole burden of this duty lies upon the shoulders of the minister.

The second circumstance is when the sick party should send for the elders to instruct him and pray for him. In the first place, the elders should be sent for before any other help is sought. Where the Divine ends, there the physician must begin. It is a very preposterous course that the Divine should there begin where the physician makes an end. Until help is found for the soul, and sin which is the root of sickness be cured, physical help for the body is worthless. It is a thing much to be disliked, that almost always the physician is sent for first in the beginning of the sickness, and only much later, the minister comes when a man is half dead, when the sick party lies drawing on and gasping for breath, as though ministers of the gospel in these days were able to work miracles.

The second duty of the sick party is to confess his sins. As St. James says, 'Confess your sins one to another and pray one for another.' It will be said that this is to bring in again Popish shrift (confession to a priest with the expectation of absolution from him).

Answer: confession of our sins, and that unto men, was never denied of any. The only question is the manner and order of making confession. For this reason we must put a great difference between Popish confession and the confession of which St. James speaks. James requires only a confession of those sins which lie upon a man's conscience when he is sick, but the Popish doctrine requires a particular enumeration of all a man's sins. Again, St. James enjoins confession as an appropriate and convenient duty, but the Papists as a thing necessary to the remission of sins. St. James permits that confession be made to any man, and by one man to another mutually, whereas Popish confession is made only to the priest. The second duty then is that the sick party who is troubled in mind with the memory and consideration of any of his past sins or is in some way being tempted by the devil, shall freely of his own accord open his case to those who are both able and willing to help him, that he may receive comfort and die in peace of conscience.

Having considered the sick man's duty, we now consider the duties of the helpers. The first is to pray over him, that is, to pray with him in his presence, and to pray for him, presenting his very person and his whole estate to God. The prophet Elijah, the apostle Paul, and our Savior Jesus Christ used this manner of praying when they would miraculously restore temporal life. It is therefore appropriate that the same should be used also of us, that we might more effectively stir up our affections in prayer, and our compassion to the sick when we are about to entreat the Lord for the remission of their sins and for the salvation of their souls.

The second duty of him that comes as a helper is to anoint the sick party with oil. This anointing was an outward ceremony that was used with the gift of healing, which is now ceased, and therefore I omit to speak further of it [a terse and abrupt treatment of this teaching of Scripture!].

Duties to himself
We have seen the duty which the sick man owes to God. Now, the duties which he is to perform to himself are twofold. One concerns his soul and the other concerns his body. The duty concerning his soul is that he must arm and furnish himself against the immoderate fear of present death. The reason for this is plain. No matter how men by nature fear death throughout the course of their lives, in time of sickness when death approaches, this natural fear bred in the bone will show itself more glaringly, even to the extent of astonishing the senses of the sick party and sometime causing desperation. It is therefore necessary that we use means to strengthen ourselves against the fears of death. There are two sorts of means: practice and meditation.

In terms of *practice*, two must be especially noted. The first is that the sick man must not so much regard death itself as he should think on the benefits of God which are obtained after death. He must not fix his mind upon the consideration of the pangs and torments of death; instead, all his thoughts and affections must be set upon that blessed estate that is enjoined after death. He that passes over some great and deep river must not look downward to the stream of the water. If he wants to prevent fear, he must set his foot sure, and cast his eye to the bank on the far side. In the same way, he that draws near death must look over the waves of death and directly fix the eye of his faith upon eternal life.

The second practice is to look upon death through the lens of the gospel and not through the lens of the law. That is, we must not consider death as it is propounded in the law, looking upon that terrible face which the law gives to death, but consider death as it is set forth in the gospel. Death in the law is a curse and the downfall to the pit of destruction, but in the gospel it is the entrance to heaven. The law sets forth death as death, while the gospel sets forth death not as death, but only a sleep, because it speaks of death as it is altered and changed by the death of Christ. In this light, death is no death to the servants of God.

When a man shall carefully consider death in this manner, it will be a notable means to strengthen and establish himself against all immoderate fears and terrors that usually rise in sickness. There are innumerable *meditations* which serve for this purpose, but let us consider the four principle ones, which are the basis for all the rest.

The first is borrowed from the special providence of God, namely, that the death of every man, much more of every child of God, is not only foreseen, but also fore-appointed by God. Even the death deserved and procured by one's own sins, is laid upon him by God, who in that respect may be said to be the cause of every man's death. So says Hannah in 1 Samuel 2:6, 'The LORD kills and makes alive; he brings down to the grave, and brings up.'

The church of Jerusalem confessed that nothing came to pass in the death of Christ except that which the foreknowledge and eternal counsel of God had appointed (Acts 4:28). The death of every member of Christ is also foreseen and ordained by the special decree and providence of God. Further, the very circumstances of death, the time when, the place where, the manner how, the beginnings of sickness, the continuance, and the end, every symptom in the sickness, even the pangs of death, are particularly set down by the counsel of God. The very hairs of our heads are numbered, as our Savior says in Matthew 10:29 and 30, and no sparrow falls to the ground without the will of our Heavenly Father. David says excellently in Psalm 139:15-16: 'My bones are not hid from you, though I was made in a secret place, and fashioned beneath in the earth: your eyes saw me when I was without form, for in your book were all things written, which in continuance were fashioned, when there was none of them before.' In Psalm 56:8, he prays to God to 'put his tears into his bottle'. Now if it is that God has bottles for the very tears of his servants, much more has he bottles for their blood, and how much more does he respect and regard their pains and miseries with all the circumstances of sickness and death.

The careful meditation of this one point is a notable means to arm us against fear, distrust, and impatience in the time of death. David says in Psalm 39:9, 'I held my tongue and said nothing.' What was it that caused this patience in him? The cause follows in the next words, 'because you, Lord, did it.' Joseph says to his brethren in Genesis 45:5, 'Fear not, for it was the Lord that sent me before you.' Notice how Joseph is armed against impatience, grief, and discontentment by the very consideration of God's providence. In the same manner we should be confirmed against all fears and sorrows, and say with David in Psalm 116:15, 'Precious in the sight of the LORD is the death of his saints.' We must be persuaded in our hearts of this one truth, that all things in sickness and death happen to us by the providence of God, who turns all things to the good of them that love him.

The second meditation is to be borrowed from the excellent promise that God has made with respect to the death of the righteous: 'Blessed are they that die in the Lord: for they rest from their labors, and their works follow them' (Rev. 14:13). The Author of truth, who cannot lie, has spoken it. Consider that death joined with a reformed life has a promise of blessedness joined to it, and it alone will be a sufficient means to control the range of our affections and all inordinate fear of death.

Death thrusts us out of our old dwelling places, the houses of clay and earthly tabernacles of our bodies, but to what end? Living and dying in Christ we have a building given of God that is a house, not made with hands but eternal in the heavens, which is unspeakable and immortal glory. If a poor man should be commanded by a prince to put off his torn and beggarly garments, and instead to put on royal and costly robes, it would cause great rejoicing in his heart. Then what joyful news must this be to all repentant and sorrowful sinners, when the King of heaven and earth comes to them by death, and invites them to lay down their bodies as ragged and patched garments, preparing themselves to put on the princely robe of immortality? No tongue can express the excellence of this most blessed and happy estate.

The third meditation is borrowed from the state of all those who are in Christ, whether living or dying. He that dies believing in Christ dies not apart from Christ, but in him, having both his body and soul joined to Christ according the tenor of the covenant of grace. Though after death body and soul are severed from one another, neither of them is severed or disjoined from Christ. The union which is once begun in this life remains eternally. While the soul goes from the body and the body itself rots in the grave, both are still in Christ, both in the covenant, both in the favor of God as before death, and both shall again be joined together, the body by the virtue of the former union being raised to eternal life. Indeed, if this union with Christ were dissolved as the union of body and soul is, it might be some matter of discomfort and fear, but the foundation and substance of our mystical union with Christ, in respect to our bodies and souls enduring for ever, is then a matter of exceeding joy and comfort.

The fourth meditation is that God has promised his special, blessed, and comforting presence to his servants when they are sick or dying, or any way distressed. The Lord said in Isaiah 43:2: 'When you pass through the waters, I will be with you; and when you pass through the rivers, they will not sweep over you. When you walk through the fire, you will not be burned; the flames will not set you ablaze.'

Now the Lord manifests his presence in three ways. First, he moderates and lessens the pains and torments of sickness and death, as the very words of the former promise plainly imply. Because of this, for many, the sorrows and pangs of death are nowhere near as difficult as the afflictions and crosses which are laid on them in the course of their lives.

The second way God's presence is manifested is by an inward and unspeakable comfort of the Spirit, as Paul says in Romans 5:3 and 5, 'We rejoice in tribulation, knowing that tribulation brings forth patience.' But why this rejoicing? Because, he says in the next words, 'the love of God is shed abroad in our hearts by the Holy Ghost.' Again, Paul having in some serious illness received the sentence of death, says of himself in 2 Corinthians 1:5: 'as the suffering of Christ abounded in our lives, so also his consolation abounds through Christ.' Here we see that when earthly comforts fail, the Lord himself draws near the bed of the sick and ministers to them refreshment for their souls, as if he were visiting them in his own person. With his left hand he holds up their heads, and with his right hand he embraces them (Song of Solomon 2:6).

The third way God's presence is made manifest is through the ministry of good angels, whom the Lord has appointed as keepers of his servants to hold them up and to bear them in their arms as nurses do young children, and to guard them against the devil and his angels. All this is verified especially in sickness, at which time the holy angels are not only present with those who fear God, but ready also to receive and carry their souls into heaven. This is apparent in the example of Lazarus.

The first duty a sick man is to perform for himself is to arm and strengthen himself against the fear of death by all possible means. Now follows the second duty, which concerns the body. All sick persons must be careful to preserve their health and life until God takes it away completely. Paul says in Romans 14:7-8: 'None of us lives to himself, neither does any die to himself; for if we live, we live unto the Lord, and if we die, we die unto the Lord.' Whether we live or die, we are the Lord's. For this reason we may not do with our lives as we will, but must entrust our whole disposition to God, for whose glory we are to live and die. This temporary life is a most precious jewel. As the common saying tells, 'Life is very sweet,' because it is given to us to the end that we might use the time entrusted to us so by all good means we might attain life everlasting. Life is not bestowed on us that we should spend our days in our lusts and vain pleasures, but that we might have liberty to come out of the kingdom of darkness into the kingdom of grace, and from the bondage of sin into the glorious liberty of the sons of God. In this respect, special care must be taken toward the preservation of life, until God calls us away from this life.

In this preserving of life, two things must be considered: the means and the right use of this means. The means is good and wholesome medicine and medical care, which, although is despised by some as unprofitable and unnecessary, must be esteemed as an ordinance and blessing of God. The Spirit of God has affirmed its use in the Scriptures. When it was the good pleasure of God to restore life unto King Hezekiah, a poultice of dry figs was applied to his boil according to the prophet's instructions, and he was healed. Indeed this cure was in some sort miraculous, because he was made whole in the space of two or three days, and the third day he went up to the temple. Still, the bunch of figs was a natural and ordinary medical treatment serving to soften and ripen tumors of swellings in the flesh. The Samaritan is commended for binding up the wounds of the man who lay dying between Jerusalem and Jericho, and for pouring wine and oil upon those wounds. This was an appropriate form of medical care. The wine served to cleanse the wound and to ease the pain within, and the oil served to supple the flesh and to assuage the pain from the outside.

The prophet Isaiah seems to commend medicine when he says in Isaiah 1:6: 'From the sole of the foot to the head, there is nothing whole, but wounds and swellings, and sores full of corruption. They have not been wrapped nor bound up, nor mollified with oil.' God did not command the circumcision of children before the eighth day, because he followed a principle of medicine observed in all ages, that the life of the child is very uncertain until after the first seven days are past, as we see by the example of the child David had by Bathsheba, who died the seventh day. For this same reason heathen men would not name their children before the eighth day. So it is seen that the use of medicine and proper medical care is lawful and commendable.

In order that medicine may be well applied toward the maintenance of health, special care must taken that physicians who are sought out are known to be well learned, men of experience, good conscience, and good religion. For as in other callings, there are numerous abuses in medical care which may endanger the lives and the health of those who receive that care. For example, some center upon the bare inspection of the patient's urine and without further direction or knowledge of the state of the sick, they prescribe and treat the illness as seems best to them based on that evaluation alone. Those experienced in proper medical care affirm that this kind of diagnosis tends to kill rather than to cure.

There are others who think it is a small matter to experiment in the treatment of their patients with medicines they have developed. By doing so, the health they hoped for is often significantly hindered, deteriorated, or decayed. There are others whose only medical treatment is blood-letting, which has on occasion killed the patient. For these reasons, those who are sick should be as careful in the selection of their physicians, to whom they might commend the care of their health, as they are careful in the selection of their lawyers for their worldly suits, and ministers for spiritual needs.

Furthermore, all must be warned against pursuing unwarranted means toward the restoration or maintenance of their health: charms; spells; characters or figures of paper, wood, or wax; and anything tied to the body or hung from the neck (unless there is some good justification for it: such as white peony hung about the neck, which is a good remedy for the falling sickness; or wolf dung tied to the body, which is a good remedy for colic). These sorts of things are all vain and superstitious, because they have no power to cure any bodily disease. Nevertheless, they are sought after and used more often by common people than is reliable, proven medicine. It would be better for a man to die of his sickness than to seek a cure from those who peddle such wicked means. If any pursue those who offer treatment through spiritism, the Lord will set his face against them, and cut them off from among his people (Lev. 20:6). When Ahaziah was sick, he sent to Beelzebub the god of Ekron to know whether he should recover or not. As the messengers were going, the prophet Elijah met them, and said in 2 Kings 1:6: 'Go and return to the king which sent you, and say unto him, thus says the LORD, "Is it because there is no God in Israel that you send to inquire of Beelzebub the god of Ekron? Therefore you shall not come down from your bed on which you are gone up, but shall die the death."' This kind of help, rather than curing any pain or sickness, doubles and fastens it upon us.

From the means of health we now turn our attention to the three principles to be followed in using the means.

First of all, the one that seeks medical attention must not only prepare his body, as the physician prescribes, but must also prepare his soul by humbling himself under the hand of God in his sickness for his sins, and must pray earnestly to God for the pardon of his sins before any medicine comes into his body.

This is because our sickness springs from our sins as from a root, which must first be pulled up, so that the branches might die more easily. In this connection, King Asa was judged by the Holy Ghost ((2 Chron. 16:12). Instead of seeking help from the Lord, King Asa sought help only from his physicians and put his trust in them alone. It often happens that diseases which are curable in themselves are made incurable by the sins and the impenitence of the diseased person. The best way to find relief and deliverance from illness that God has sent to correct us is to begin to humble ourselves for all our sins and turn to our God.

The second principle is that once we have prepared ourselves and are about to seek medical attention, we must sanctify the medical care by the Word of God and prayer, as we do our food and drink. By the Word we must validate the legitimacy of the medical care prescribed, and by prayer we must entreat the Lord for a blessing upon it, toward the restoration of health, if it is the good and perfect will of God.

The third principle is that we must carry in mind the right and proper end of medical care so that we do not deceive ourselves. We must not think that medicine serves to prevent old age or death itself. That is not possible, because God has proclaimed that all men shall die and be changed. The true end of medicine is to continue and lengthen the life of man to its natural end, when nature has been preserved as long as possible by all possible means, and is now wholly spent. While length of life cannot be extended by any skill of man, it may easily be shortened by an unhealthy diet, by drunkenness, and by violent diseases. Care must be taken to avoid all such evils, so that the little lamp of our bodily life may burn until it goes out by itself. This space of time is the very day of grace and salvation. Where God in justice might have cut us off and utterly destroyed us, in great mercy he gives us a certain amount of time so that we might prepare ourselves for his kingdom; when that time is spent, if a man would seek to buy more with the price of ten thousand worlds he cannot have it.

Finally, to conclude this point dealing with medical care, let us consider two special duties of the physician himself. First, in the absence or inability of one who may put a sick man in mind of his sins, it is the special duty of the physician, being a member of Christ, to challenge his patients that they must truly humble themselves, and pray fervently to God for the pardon of all their sins. Surely this duty would be more commonly practiced than it is if all physicians considered and understood that often they lack success in their treatment of patients, not because of lacking ability or good intentions on their part, but because the patient whom they are treating is unrepentant.

The second duty is that when he sees evidence that death is approaching, he must not conceal that fact from his patient, but tell him plainly. There may be some benefit or appearance of compassion in such concealment, but the plain truth regarding the patient's condition is always more profitable to the patient himself. For when the party is certain of his end, it bereaves him of all confidence in earthly things, and makes him put all his trust and confidence in the mercy of God. When Hezekiah was sick, the prophet spoke to him plainly, 'Set your house in order, for you must die' (Isa. 38:1). Knowing for certain that we are under the sentence of death is a great benefit to us, for Paul says in 2 Corinthians 1:9: 'We have received the sentence of death in ourselves, because we should not trust in ourselves, but in God which raises the dead.'

Duties to his neighbor

Having considered the duties of the sick man to himself, let us now consider the two duties he owes to his neighbor. The first is the duty of *reconciliation*, by which he is to forgive all men freely and to desire to be forgiven of all. In the Old Testament, when a man was to offer a bull or lamb in sacrifice to God, he was to leave his offering at the altar, and first go and be reconciled to his brethren, if they had anything against him. Much more, then, must this be done when we are about to offer up ourselves, our bodies, and our souls in death, as an acceptable sacrifice to God.

Question: What if a man cannot contact or speak to those with whom he seeks reconciliation. If he does speak with them, what if they refuse to be reconciled?

Answer: when in their sickness they shall seek and desire reconciliation, and cannot obtain it, either because the parties are absent or because they will not relent, they have discharged their conscience, and God will accept their will or intentions for the deed. For example, a man lying sick on his death bed is in conflict with one that is then beyond the sea so he can't possibly have any communication with him, even if he greatly desires to be reconciled to him. How can he calm his mind? He must remember that in this case, a will and desire to be reconciled is reconciliation itself.

The second duty is that those which are rulers and governors of others must make certain that the charges committed to them by God are left in a good state after their death. This applies especially to the roles of magistrate, minister, and master of the family. The magistrate's duty before he dies is to provide as much as he can for the godly and peaceable state of the town, city, or commonwealth. This is done partly by providing for the maintenance of sound religion and virtue, and partly by establishing the execution of civil justice and outward peace. Examples of this practice are found in God's Word.

When Moses was a hundred and twenty years old and was no longer able to go in and out before the people of Israel, he called them before him, and told them that the time of his departure was at hand. He then arranged for their welfare after his death. He begins by placing Joshua over them in his stead, to be their guide to the promised land. Then, he gives special charge to all the people, to be valiant and courageous against their enemies, and to obey the commandments of God.

Joshua follows the same course in Joshua 23, when he calls the people together, shows them that the time of his death is at hand, and gives them a charge to be courageous and to worship the true God. Having done this, he ends his days as a worthy captain.

When King David lay sick on his deathbed and was about to go the way of all flesh, he placed his own son Solomon upon his throne and charged him toward the maintenance of religion and the execution of justice.

The duty of ministers when they are dying is to call and provide for the continuance of the good estate of the church over which they are placed. Consider the example of Peter, in 2 Peter 1:15: 'I will endeavor always that you also may be able to have remembrance of these things after my departure.' If this had been well observed, there could not have been so many schisms, errors, and heresies as have been, and the church of God could not have suffered such great conflict. Because men have placed more emphasis on maintaining personal succession than on maintaining the right succession, which stands in the doctrine of the prophets and apostles, wolves have come into the room of faithful teachers and have spread throughout the church.

Third, heads of households must set their families in order before they die, as the prophet Isaiah says to Hezekiah, 'Set your house in order for you must die' (2 Kings 20:1). In order to ensure good order in the family after one's death, two things are to be done. The first, concerning this life, is to dispose of lands and goods. Of greatest importance in this connection is to have a last will and testament prepared. If one is lacking before the onset of illness, it is with godly advice and counsel to be made in the time of sickness, according to the practice of ancient and worthy men. Before he died, Abraham made his will and left legacies, as did Isaac, and Jacob, in whose last will and testament are contained many worthy blessings and prophecies of the estate of his children. Even our Savior Jesus Christ, in John 19:27, provided for his mother when he was upon the cross, specifically commending her to his disciple John, whom he loved. Indeed, this duty of making a will is a matter of great weight and importance, for it cuts off much hatred and contention in families, and prevents many law suits. Preparing a will, therefore, is not a matter of indifference, as many falsely think, even for those who refuse to prepare a will because their wealth should not be known, because they wish to conceal a decayed estate, or because they fear they shall die sooner once the will is made.

Though the making of wills belongs to another place and profession, much may be spoken as the Holy Ghost has uttered in the Word, which may be reduced to certain principles.

The first is that the will must be made according to the law of nature, the written Word of God, and the good and wholesome positive laws of that kingdom or country of which a man is a member. The will of God must be the rule of man's will, and, therefore, the will that is prepared in a way that ignores God's will is faulty.

The second principle is, that if goods acquired through evil means have not been restored before the time of death, they must be restored, either by the will or by some other way. It is the practice of courteous men to bequeath their souls to God when they die, and their goods gotten through evil means to their children and friends, which in all fairness should be restored to those to whom they belong.

Question: what if a man's conscience convicts him that his property has been obtained in an evil manner, but he doesn't know to whom to make restitution, or where?

Answer: this is a common case, and is resolved as follows. When the wronged party is known, restore his particular property to him; if the party is unknown or dead, restore to his executors or assignees, or to his next of kin. If there is no next of kin, still, do not keep such property for yourself or for your family. Instead, restore it to God. In way of recompense and civil satisfaction, bestow those things on the church or community.

The third principle is that heads of families must principally bestow their goods upon their own children, and those of their extended family. In Genesis 15:4, God said to Abraham about Eliezer, a stranger, 'This man shall not be your heir, but the son which shall come of your loins.' God's commandment to the Israelites was when any man dies, his son should be his heir; and if he has no son, then his daughter; and if he has no daughter, then his brethren; and if he has no brethren, then his father's brethren; and if there are none, then the next of his kin whomever that may be.

Paul says in Romans 8:17, 'If you be sons, then also heirs.' Again in 1 Timothy 5:8, he says: 'He that provides not for his own, namely for them of his household, has denied the faith and is worse than an infidel.' It is wrong for any man to alienate his goods or lands, wholly and finally, from his blood and posterity; this is something that the very law of nature itself has condemned. Again, it is a fault to give all to the eldest, and nothing in respect to the rest, as though the eldest were born to be gentlemen, and younger brethren born to bear the wallet. Yet in all fairness, the eldest must have more than the others, specifically because he is the eldest, and because flocks and families are to be specially maintained by them. This is also true because there must always be some that are fit to do special service in the peace of the community, or in time of war; this could not be if goods were equally parted to all.

The fourth and last principle is that no will is in force until the testator be dead, for as long as he is alive, he may alter and change it. These principles must be remembered, because they are recorded in Scripture. The further explanation of other details and unusual circumstances in this connection belong to the profession of the law.

The second duty of the master of the family concerns the souls of those under his government. He is to exercise his authority in such a way that they learn, believe, and obey the true religion – the doctrine of salvation set down in the writings of the prophets and apostles. The Lord himself commended Abraham for this: 'I have chosen him, so that he will direct his children and his household after him to keep the way of the LORD by doing what is right and just, so that the LORD will bring about for Abraham what he has promised him.'

David, when on his deathbed, gives Solomon a most notable and solemn charge, the basis of which was to know the God of his fathers, and to serve him. Having done this, he further commends Solomon to God by prayer, for which purpose the 72nd Psalm was written.

This practice is to be followed by all, for in this way, when heads of households carefully dispose of their goods, and challenge their posterity in their proper worship of God, they will greatly honor God, dying, as well as living.

Disposition in death
From the preparation which precedes death, we turn our attention to the second part of dying well, which is the disposition in death. This disposition is a religious and holy behavior, especially towards God, when we are in or near the agony of death. This behavior contains three special duties.

The first is to die *in or by faith*. To die by faith is when a man in the time of death entrusts himself with all his heart wholly on God's special love, favor, and mercy in Christ, as it is revealed in the Word. Though there is no part of man's life where the occasion to put faith in practice is absent, the critical time is at the agony of death, when friends, riches, pleasures, the outward senses of this life, and all earthly helps forsake us. This true faith makes us go wholly outside of ourselves, to despair of comfort and salvation in respect of any earthly thing, and with all the power and strength of the heart, to rest on the pure mercy of God. This made Luther say that men were best Christians in death. We have an example of this faith in David, who when he saw nothing before his eyes but immanent death, the people intending to stone him, he comforted himself at that very instant in the Lord his God. He reaped this comfort by applying to his own soul the merciful promises of God, as he testifies of himself in Psalm 119:49: 'Remember your word to your servant, for you have given me hope. My comfort in my suffering is this: your promise preserves my life.' Again, Asaph says in Psalm 73:26: 'My flesh failed and my heart also, but God is the strength of my heart, and my portion for ever.'

What these psalmists did here is what every one of us must do when we encounter such a time and situation. When the Israelites were bitten by fiery serpents in the wilderness and lay at the point of death, they looked up to the brazen serpent which was erected by the appointment of God, and were presently healed. Even so, when any man feels death drawing near and its fiery sting piercing his heart, he must fix the eye of a true and lively faith upon Christ, exalted and crucified on the cross, which being done, he shall by death enter into eternal life.

Because true faith is no dead thing, it must be expressed by special actions. This begins with invocation, by which either prayer or thanksgiving is directed to God. When death had seized upon the body of Jacob, he raised himself up, and turning his face towards the bed's head, leaned on the top of his staff because of his feebleness, and prayed to God a prayer which was an excellent fruit of his faith. In the midst of his affliction, Job's wife said to him, 'Bless God and die.' I know and grant that the words are commonly translated otherwise, 'Curse God and die,' but, as I take it, the former is better. It is unlikely that in such an excellent family any one person, much less the wife and mother in the home, would give such lewd and wretched counsel that even the most wicked man upon earth, having only the light of nature to guide him, would not give. Though Job called her a foolish woman, he does it not because she sought to persuade him to blaspheme God, but because she was of the mind of Job's friends and thought that he stood too much in a conceit of his own righteousness. The very meaning of her counsel is this: 'Bless God, that is, husband, no doubt you art by the extremity of your affliction at death's door; therefore, begin now to set aside your high view of your own righteousness, acknowledge the hand of God upon you for your sins, confess them to him, give him the glory, pray for the pardon of your sins, and end your days.' This counsel is very good and to be followed by all, though, even as Job perceived, the applying of it may be mixed with folly.

It may be objected that in the pangs of death men lack their clear senses and even the ability to speak and are, therefore, unable to pray.

Answer: the very sighs, sobs, and groans of a repentant and believing heart are prayers before God, even as effectual as if they were uttered by the best voice in the world. Prayer stands in the affection of the heart, of which the voice is but an outward messenger. God looks not upon the speech, but upon the heart. David says, 'God hears the desires of the poor,' and that 'he will fulfill the desires of them that fear him; yea their very tears are loud and sounding praise in his ears.'

Faith may otherwise be expressed by the last words, which, in those that have truly served God are very excellent, comfortable, and full of grace. Some choice examples of this may be cited for instruction's sake and for imitation.

The last words of Jacob were when as a prophet he foretold blessings and cursings upon his children. The main words of this as it reads in Genesis 49 are: 'The scepter shall not depart from Judah, and the law-giver from between his feet, till Shiloh come;' and 'O LORD, I have waited for your salvation.' The last words of Moses are set down in his most excellent song in Deuteronomy 31.

The last words of David were recorded in 2 Samuel 23:2: 'The Spirit of the LORD spoke by me, and his Word was in my tongue: the God of Israel spoke to me, the strength of Israel said, Bear rule over me.'

The last words of Zechariah, the son of Jehoida, when he was stoned were, 'The Lord look upon it, and requite it' (2 Chron. 24:22).

The last words of our Savior Jesus Christ, when he was dying upon the cross, were most admirable, rich with an abundance of spiritual grace.

1. To his Father: 'Father, forgive them, they know not what they do' (Luke 23:34).

2. To the thief: 'Verily, I say unto you, this day shall you be with me in Paradise' (Luke 23:43).

3. To his mother: 'Mother, behold your son' (John 19:26); to John: 'Behold your mother' (John 19:27).

4. In his agony: 'My God, my God, why have you forsaken me?' (Mark 15:34).

5. Earnestly desiring our salvation: 'I thirst' (John 19:28).

6. When he had made perfect satisfaction: 'It is finished' (John 19:30).

7. When body and soul were parting: 'Father, into your hands, I commend my spirit' (Luke 23:46).

The last words of Stephen: (a) 'Behold, I see the heaven open, and the Son of man standing at the right hand of God' (Acts 7:56); (b) 'Lord Jesus, receive my spirit' (Acts 7:59); (c) 'Lord, lay not this sin to their charge' (Acts 7:60).

The last words of Polycarp: 'You are a true God without lying, therefore in all things I praise you and bless you, and glorify you by the eternal God, and High Priest Jesus Christ, your only beloved Son, by whom, and with whom, to you and the Holy Spirit, be all glory now and forever.'

The last words of Ignatius: 'I care not what kind of death I die: I am the bread of the Lord, and must be ground with the teeth of lions, that I may be clean bread for Christ who is the bread of life for me.'

The last words of Ambrose: 'I have not led my life among you, as if I were ashamed to live; neither do I fear death, because we have a good Lord.'

The last words of Augustine: (a) 'He is no great man that thinks it is a great matter, that trees and stones fall, and mortal men die; (b) Just are you, O Lord, and righteous in your judgment.'

The last words of Bernard: 1. An admonition to his brethren that they would ground the anchor of their faith and hope in the safe and sure port of God's mercy. 2. 'As I suppose I cannot leave unto you any choice example of religion, I commend three things to be imitated of you, which I remember that I have observed in the race which I have run as much as possibly I could: (a) I gave less heed to mine own sense and reason, than to the sense and reason of other men; (b) When I was hurt, I sought no revenge on him that did the hurt; (c) I had care to give offense to no man, and if it fell out otherwise, I took it away as I could.'

The last words of Ulrich Zwingli, when in the field he was wounded under the chin with a spear: 'O what a happy day is this! They may kill my body, but my soul they cannot.'

The last words of Johannes Oecolampadius (sixteenth century German Reformer whose life and ministry coincided with Luther and Zwingli):

1. An exhortation to the ministers of the church to maintain the purity of doctrine, to show forth an example of home and godly conversation, and to be constant and patient under the cross.
2. Of himself, 'Whereas I am charged to be a corrupter of the truth, I weigh it not. Now I am going to the tribunal of Christ, and that with good conscience by the grace of God, and there it shall be manifest that I have not seduced the church. Of this my saying and contesting, I leave you as witnesses, and I confirm it with this my last breath.'
3. To his children, 'Love God the Father.'
4. Turning himself to his kinsfolk, 'I have bound you with this contestation: "you shall do your endeavor, that these my children may be godly, and peaceable, and true."'
5. To his friends coming to him, 'What shall I say unto you? News: I shall be shortly with Christ my Lord.'
6. When asked whether the light troubled him, touching his breast, he said, 'There is light enough.'
7. He rehearsed the whole 51st Psalm with deep sighs from the bottom of his breast.
8. A little after, 'Save me, Lord Jesus.'

The last words of Luther: 'My heavenly Father, God and Father of our Lord Jesus Christ, and God of all comfort, I give you thanks that you have revealed unto me your Son, Jesus Christ, whom I have blessed, whom I have professed, whom the Bishop of Rome, and the whole company of the wicked, distort and confuse. I pray you, my Lord Jesus Christ, receive my poor soul. My heavenly

Father, though I be taken from this life, and this body of mine is to be laid down, yet I know certainly that I shall remain with you for ever, neither shall any be able to pull me out of your hand.'

The last words of Hooper: 'O Lord Jesus, son of David have mercy on me, and receive my soul.'

The last words of Anna Burgins: 'Forsake me not, O Lord, lest I forsake you.'

The last words of Melancthon: 'If it be the will of God, I am willing to die, and I beseech him that he will grant me a joyful departure.'

The last words of Calvin: (a) 'I held my tongue, because you Lord, have done it;' (b) 'I mourned as a dove;' (c) 'Lord you grind me to powder, but it suffices me because it is your hand.'

The last words of Peter Martyr: his body was weak, but his mind was well; he acknowledged no life or salvation, but only in Christ who was given of the Father to be a Redeemer of mankind; and when he had confirmed this by testimony of Scripture, he added, 'This is my faith in which I will die, and God will destroy them that teach otherwise.' This done he shook hands with all and said, 'Farewell, my brethren, and dear friends.'

It would be possible to quote many more examples, but these few may suffice instead of many. The sum of all that godly men speak, is as follows.

Some enlightened with a prophetic Spirit foretell things to come, as the Patriarchs, Jacob and Joseph did. There have been some who by name have testified who should very shortly come after them, and who should remain alive, and what should be their condition.

Some have showed a wonderful memory of things past, as of their former life, and of the benefits of God, and no doubt it was given them to stir up holy affections and thanksgiving to God.

Some, rightly judging of the change of their present estate for a better one, rejoice greatly that they must be translated from earth to paradise, as Babylas, Martyr of Antioch, said when he was to be beheaded: 'Return, O my soul unto your rest, because the Lord has blessed you. Because God has delivered my soul from death, mine eyes from tears, and my feet from falling, I shall walk before you, Jehovah, in the land of the living.'

Others spoke of the vanity of this life, of the imagination of the sorrows of death, of the beginning of eternal life, of the comfort of the Holy Ghost which they feel, and of their departure unto Christ.

Question: What must we think if in the time of death that kind of thinking and speech are absent, and instead, idle talk is used?

Answer: we must consider the kind of sickness of which men die, whether it be more easy or violent. For violent sickness is usually accompanied with frenzies and with unseemly motions and gestures, which should be taken into consideration, because we ourselves may be in such a condition.

Having considered the first duty, dying in faith, we now consider the second, which is *to die in obedience*. Apart from this our death cannot be acceptable to God, because we would be coming to God out of fear and constraint as slaves to a master, and not of love as children to a father. To die in obedience is this: a man must be willing and ready to go out of this world at whatever time God shall call him, without murmuring or complaining about the time, place, or manner that pleases God. Paul says, whether we live or die, we do it not to ourselves but unto God, and therefore, man's duty is to be obedient to God in death as in life. Christ is our example in this, for even in his agony he prayed, 'Father, let this cup pass from me,' yet with submission, 'not my will, but your will be done,' teaching us in the very pangs of death to resign ourselves to the good pleasure of God. When the prophet told King Hezekiah of death, immediately, without any grudging, he addressed himself to prayer.

We are commanded to present ourselves unto God as free will offerings, without any limitation of time, in death as well as in life. I conclude then, that we are to make as much of a conscientious effort in performing obedience to God in suffering death, as we do of anything in the course of our lives.

The third duty is *to render up our souls into the hands of God*, as the most faithful keeper of all. This is the last duty of a Christian, and it is prescribed to us by the example of Christ upon the cross, who in the very pangs of death, when the separation of body and soul approached, said, 'Father, into your hands, I commend my Spirit' (Luke 23:46), and he gave up the ghost. This was also done by Stephen, who when he was stoned to death said, 'Lord Jesus receive my Spirit' (Acts 7:59). When David was in danger of death, he used the very same words that Christ uttered, 'Into your hand I commit my spirit' (Ps. 31:5).

Thus we see the duties which we are to perform in the very pangs of death that we may assuredly come into eternal life. Some men will glibly say, 'If this is all there is to dying in faith and in obedience, and to surrender our souls into God's hands, we will not concern ourselves with any preparation beforehand, nor trouble ourselves much about the right manner of dying well. For when death shall come, we shall be able to perform all the former duties with ease.'

Answer: let no man deceive himself by any false persuasion, thinking to himself that the practice of these final duties is a matter of ease, for ordinarily they are not. They cannot be performed in death, unless there is preparation in the life before.

He that will die in faith must first of all live by faith. There is but one example in all the Bible of a man dying in faith that lived without faith, namely, the thief upon the cross. Even the servants of God who are blessed with a great measure of grace sometimes struggle with clinging to their faith in the time of affliction. Indeed, when Job was afflicted he said, 'Though the Lord kill me, yet will I trust in him.' Afterward, when his faith was overcast with a cloud, he said that God had become his enemy, and that he had become a target to shoot at. Numerous times his faith was oppressed with doubting and distrust.

How then shall they that never lived by faith, nor acquainted themselves with true belief, be able to rest upon the mercy of God in the pangs of death? Again, he that would die in obedience must first of all lead his life in obedience. He that lived in disobedience cannot willingly and in obedience appear before the judge when he is cited by death, the sergeant of the Lord. He dies indeed, but this is upon necessity, because he must yield to the order and course of nature, as other creatures do.

He that would surrender his soul into the hands of God must be resolved of two things. One is that God can receive his soul into heaven; the other is that God will receive his soul into heaven, and there preserve it till the last judgment. None can be resolved of this, unless he has the Spirit of God to certify to his conscience that he is redeemed, justified, sanctified by Christ, and shall be glorified. He that is not thus persuaded dare not render up and present his soul unto God. When David said in Psalm 31:5, 'LORD, into your hands I commend my Spirit,' what was the reason of this boldness in him? Surely nothing else was reason at all but the persuasion of which he speaks in the next word, 'For you have redeemed me, O LORD God of truth.'

It must be clearly recognized that no man can ordinarily perform the right duties in dying that he has not performed while living. This being so, I do again renew my former exhortation, pleading with you to practice the duties of preparation throughout the course of your lives, pursuing them daily in faith and obedience, from time to time commending your souls into the hand of God, and casting all your works upon his providence. They who have done this have prepared for the most happy and blessed end of life. Enoch walked with God by faith, as one that was always in his presence, leading an upright and godly life, and the Lord took him away that he should not see death. What happened to Enoch will eventually happen to all those who live in faith and obedience, because death shall be no death, but only a sleep to them, and therefore, death shall be no enemy but a friend to body and soul.

On the contrary, let us consider the wretched and miserable ends of those who spend their days in their sins without keeping faith and good conscience. The people of the old world were drowned in the flood. The filthy Sodomites and Gomorraheans were destroyed with fire from heaven. Dathan and Abiram, along with the company of Korah, were swallowed up by the earth, Korah himself being burned with fire. Wicked Saul, Ahithophel, and Judas destroy themselves in suicide. Herod was eaten up of worms and gave up the ghost. Julian the Apostle, hit by a dart in the field, died casting up his blood into the air and blaspheming the name of Christ. Arius the heretic died upon the stool, scouring forth his very entrails.

Even this very age provides us with similar examples. Hoffmeister, a great Papist, as he was going to the Council of Ratisbone to dispute with the defenders of the gospel, was suddenly prevented by the hand of God and miserably died with horrible roaring and crying out.

In the University of Louaine, Guarlacus, a learned Papist, became sick, and when he perceived no way with him but death, fell into a miserable agony of spirit, crying out of his sins, how miserably he had lived, and that he was not able to abide the judgment of God. Then casting out words of miserable desperation, he said his sins were greater than could be pardoned, and in that desperation ended his days.

Jacobus Latomus of the same University of Louaine, after attempting to do a great act against Luther and his fellows, made an oration before the Emperor so foolishly and ridiculously that he was laughed at and scorned by the whole court. Returning from there to Louaine again, he fell into open madness during his public lecture, uttering such words of desperation and blasphemous impiety, that other Divines who were present were forced to carry him away as he was raving, and shut him into a closed chamber. From that time to his very last breath, he had never anything else in his mouth, except that he was damned and rejected of God, and that there was no hope of salvation for him, because he had knowingly withstood the manifest truth of God's Word.

Crescentius, the Pope's Legate and Vicegerent in the Council of Trent, was sitting all day long until dark night, writing letters to the Pope. That night, thinking to refresh himself, he began to rise, and there appeared to him a huge, mighty black dog, his eyes flaming with fire, and his ears hanging down well near to the ground. The dog entered his room and began to come toward him. The Cardinal, not a little amazed at the sight, called to his servants who were in the outward chamber, to bring a candle and to search for the dog. When the dog could not be found there, nor in any other chamber, the Cardinal was immediately stricken with a sickness of which his physicians could not, with all their industry and cunning, cure him, and he died.

When a certain Bishop came to Stephen Gardiner and spoke with him of Peter denying his master, he answered that he had denied with Peter, but never repented with Peter. In that state, he stingingly and unrepentantly died. More examples might be added, but these shall suffice.

Again, that we may be further challenged and motivated to practice these duties, let us call to mind the uncertainty of our days. Though we now live, who can say that he shall be alive the next day or the next hour? No man has a lease on his life. Note well, as death leaves a man, so shall the last judgment find him. Therefore, if death take him away unprepared, eternal damnation follows without recovery. If a thief is brought from prison to the court to be tried before the judge, or to the place of execution, he will bewail his past, and promise all reformation of life. In some cases he might be delivered, though he be the most errant thief that ever was. In this case we are as felons or thieves. For we are every day going to the courtroom of God's judgment.

There is no stay or standing in the way, even as the ship in the sea continues on its course day and night whether the sailors are sleeping or waking. Therefore, let us all prepare ourselves, and amend our lives over time, that in death we may make a blessed end. Ministers of the gospel must daily call for the performance of this duty. But where shall we find the practice and obedience of it in men's lives and conversation? Alas, to lend our ears for the space of an hour to hear the will of God is common; but to give heart and hand to do the same is rare, for this reason: we are all most grievous sinners, and every sinner in the terms of Scripture is a fool. At the center of this folly is to care for the things of this world, to neglect the kingdom of heaven, to provide for the body and not for the soul, to cast and forecast how we may live in wealth and honor and ease, and not to use the least forecast to die well.

Our Savior Jesus Christ noted this folly in the rich man that was careful to enlarge his barns, but had no care at all for his end or for the salvation of his soul. Such a one was Ahithophel who was as the very voice of God for counsel, being a man of great wisdom and forecast in the matters of the commonwealth and in his own private worldly affairs. Yet for all this he had not so much as common sense and reason to consider how he might die the death of the righteous and come to life everlasting. This folly is pointed out by the Holy Ghost in 2 Samuel 17:23, for 'when Ahithophel saw that his counsel was despised, he saddled his donkey, rode home into his city, put his household in order, and went and hanged himself.'

The five foolish virgins contented themselves with the blazing lamps of bare profession, never seeking for the horn of lasting oil of true and lively faith, that it might furnish and trim the lamp both in life and death. Let us, in the fear of God, cast off this damnable folly, seeking the kingdom of God and his righteousness, and leading our lives in faith and obedience, that we may die accordingly.

An addition of things that came to my mind afterward: the last combat with the devil in the final throes of death is often the most dangerous of all. Then he will not urge men to desperation, knowing that by this means he shall stir them up to resist. Instead he labors with them that they would not resist him when he assaults them, and by this means he endeavors to extinguish hope. This is not done in any other temptation in which faith or hope alone are attacked, whereas in this they are both attacked together. This must be carefully considered, for when the devil's temptation is to not resist his temptation, it is most deceitful of all. It is easier to overcome the enemy that compels us to fight than him that dissuades us from it.

The temptation of John Knox in the time of his death is worth the marking. He lay on his deathbed silent for the space of four hours, very often giving great signs, sobs, and groans, so that the bystanders clearly perceived that he was troubled with some grievous temptation. When at length he was raised in his bed, he said that in his lifetime he had endured many combats and conflicts with Satan, but that it was now that the roaring lion had assaulted him most mightily. He went on to say, 'Often before he set my sins before mine eyes; often he urged me to desperation, often he labored to entangle me with the delights of the world; but being vanquished by the Sword of the Spirit, which is the Word of God, he could not prevail. But now he assaults me another way, for the wily serpent would persuade me that I shall merit eternal life for my fidelity in my ministry. But blessed be God who brought to my mind such Scriptures by which I might quench the fiery darts of the devil, which were, "What have you that you have not received?" and, "By the grace of God, I am that I am," and, "Not I but the grace of God in me." Thus being vanquished he departed.'

When you are tempted by Satan and see no way to escape, close your eyes, and answer nothing, but commend your cause to God.

This is a principal point of Christian wisdom which we must follow in the hour of death.

Martin Luther has written: 'If your flesh trembles and fears to enter into another life, and you doubt your salvation, if you yield to these things, you wound yourself. Therefore, close your eyes as before, and say with Stephen, "Lord Jesus, into your hands I commend my Spirit," and Christ will certainly come to you with all his angels, and be the guide of your way.'

BIBLIOGRAPHY

Ames, William. *Conscience with the Power and Cases.* London: Microfilm, 1641.

Baxter, Richard. *A Christian Directory,* 4 vols. Ligonier, PA: Soli Deo Gloria Publications,1990.

Baxter, Richard. *The Reformed Pastor.* 1656. Reprint, Edinburgh: Banner of Truth Trust, 1983.

Brook, Benjamin. *The Lives of the Puritans,* 3 vols. 1813. Reprint, Morgan, PA: Soli Deo Gloria Publications, 1994.

Byington, Ezra Hoyt. *The Puritan in England and New England.* Boston: Roberts Brothers, 1897.

Crabb, Larry. *The Silence of Adam.* Grand Rapids, MI: Zondervan, 1995.

Davies, Samuel. 'The Necessity and Excellence of Family Religion.' In *The Godly Family.* Pittsburgh, PA: Soli Deo Gloria Publications, 1993.

Dennison, James T. Jr. *The Market Day of the Soul: The Puritan Doctrine of the Sabbath in England 1532–1700.* New York: University Press of America, 1983. Quoted in Joseph A. Pipa, *The Lord's Day* (Great Britian: Christian Focus Publications, 1997), p. 42.

Doriani, Daniel. 'The Godly Household in Puritan Theology, 1560–1640' (Th.D. diss., Westminster Theological Seminary, 1986), *University Microfilms International* (1986).

Edwards, Jonathan. *The Works of Jonathan Edwards.* Edinburgh: The Banner of Truth Trust,1992.

Gataker, Thomas. *Certaine Sermons,* Vol. 2 (London: J. Haviland, 1635), p. 206. Quoted in Daniel Doriani, 'The Godly Household in Puritan Theology, 1560–1640' (Th.D. diss., Westminster Theological Seminary, 1986), *University Microfilms International* (1986), p. 268.

Gouge, William. *Of Domestical Duties.* London: Facsimile, 1622.

Ireland, David. *Letters to an Unborn Child.* New York, NY: Harper & Rowe, 1974.

Murray, Ian. *Jonathan Edwards: A New Biography*. Edinburgh: The Banner of Truth Trust,1987.

Packer, J. I. *A Quest for Godliness: The Puritan Vision of the Christian Life*. Wheaton: Crossway Books, 1990.

Perkins, William, *A Salve for a Sicke Man, or The Right Manner of Dying Well*. London: University of Cambridge, Microfilm, 1616.

Pipa, Joseph A. *The Lord's Day*. Great Britain: Christian Focus Publications, 1997.

Puritan Sermons, 1659–1689, 6 Vols. 1674. Reprint, Wheaton, Ill: Richard Owen Roberts, Publishers, 1981.

Rogers, Daniel, *Matrimonial Honour* (London: T. Harper, 1643), p. 193. Quoted in Daniel Doriani, 'The Godly Household in Puritan Theology, 1560–1640' (Th.D. diss., Westminster Theological Seminary, 1986), *University Microfilms International* (1986), p. 268.

Ryken, Leland. *Worldly Saints: The Puritans As They Really Were*. Grand Rapids, MI: Academie Books, 1986.

Westminster Confession of Faith, Suwanee, GA: Great Commission Publications, 1995.

OTHER CHRISTIAN FOCUS
TITLES OF INTEREST

WORLD-PROOF YOUR KIDS

RAISING CHILDREN UNSTAINED BY THE WORLD

TIM SISEMORE

WITH RUTH SISEMORE

World-proof Your Kids:

Raising Children Unstained by the World

Tim Sisemore with Ruth Sisemore

Many Christian parents are at their wits end about raising their children in a healthy and spiritual way. Increasingly the influence of the world, with it's 'me first' obsession, is causing problems within the Christian home.

This influence causes Christian families to fall into the four categories:

- The disillusioned family
- The distracted family
- The disciplinarian family
- The dedicated family

All end up being influenced by the culture rather than by their faith.

Is your family influenced by the culture rather than your faith. Is your family falling into an unhealthy pattern of behaviour? It's time to find out and put things right.

If you want to help your family then the Sisemore's are here to help break the cycle.

Dr Timothy Sisemore is one of America's leading child and adolescent Christian psychologists. He is the Clincal Professor of Psychology and Counselling at the Psychological Studies Institute. He maintains a clinical practice at the Chattanooga Bible Institute Counseling Center and has been published in Professional Psychology Research & Practice, The Journal for Christian Educators and the Journal of Psychology & Christianity. Ruth Sisemore is his wife and vitally helps Tim translate theory into practice!

ISBN 978-1-84550-275-1

Dr. Timothy A. Sisemore

OUR
COVENANT
with KIDS

Biblical Nurture in Home and Church

Our Covenant With Kids:

Biblical Nurture in Home and Church

Timothy Sisemore

Dr. Sisemore teaches you about – Christian parenting in a hostile world, educating children spiritually and academically, cultivating godliness, disciplining and discipling, honoring parents, how are children saved? The church's responsibility towards its children, children's involvement in worship and sacraments.

This is a practical and theological approach to parenting and children's ministry – and shows how to nurture children to be disciples.

His approach is what the Bible calls wisdom...as rich in Biblical instruction as it is in psychological insight.
> Edmund P. Clowney, Emeritus Professor of Practical Theology
> Westminster Theological Seminary

Anyone who has a true concern for the spiritual welfare of children in this present age must read this book!
> Mark Johnston, Grove Chapel, London

Underscores the need not only to teach our children about God but also to develop a worldview that enables them to see the totality of their Christian faith in all things... I recommend it as an important book.
> Charles Dunahoo
> Christian Education & Publications, Presbyterian Church in
> America

Here is a straightforward, readable, challenging and practical manual – just what parents are looking for.
> Sinclair B. Ferguson

ISBN 9781845503505

THE

BIG
BOOK

OF

BIBLE TRUTHS 1

SINCLAIR B. FERGUSON

Big Book of Bible Truths 1

Sinclair B. Ferguson

You can never have too many stories! Children love them: We all do! And who better to hear about in a story than the great storyteller himself, Jesus.

Through the stories in this book you will find out about him, his life, how he wants to get to know you. Sinclair tells twenty-seven stories that will teach you about what it means to be a Christian.

Nick-names, moth burgers – there are many interesting stories that teach you things you didn't know before – and loads of cool stuff about Jesus Christ, the Son of God.

Illustrated throughout, this book is going to be another family favourite! **Includes Extra Features**: Bible reading; lesson summary; prayer

ISBN 9781845503710

The Big Book of Bible Truths 2

THE
BIG
BOOK
OF
BIBLE TRUTHS 2

SINCLAIR B. FERGUSON

Big Book of Bible Truths 2

Sinclair B. Ferguson

We all love stories - can you ever have too many? There is no one better to hear about in a story than the greatest storyteller himself, Jesus. These stories will help you discover even more about him, his life – how he wants to get to know **you**.

Here are another twenty-seven stories that will teach you about what it means to belong to God's family. There are lots of different people to discover, including an architect and a master craftsman. You will also be able to work out what a revival is and if Jesus' mum ever got in a tizzy?

Sinclair tells many interesting stories that will teach you things you didn't know before. God, Jesus and You – what a team! Now that's a winning combination (no doubt about it!

There are illustrations throughout the book so it's all set to be another of your family's favourites! **Includes Extra Features:** Bible reading; lesson summary; prayer

ISBN 9781845003727

Christian Focus Publications
publishes books for all ages

Our mission statement –

STAYING FAITHFUL
In dependence upon God we seek to help make His infallible Word, the Bible, relevant. Our aim is to ensure that the Lord Jesus Christ is presented as the only hope to obtain forgiveness of sin, live a useful life and look forward to heaven with Him.

REACHING OUT
Christ's last command requires us to reach out to our world with His gospel. We seek to help fulfil that by publishing books that point people towards Jesus and help them develop a Christ-like maturity. We aim to equip all levels of readers for life, work, ministry and mission.

Books in our adult range are published in three imprints.

Christian Focus contains popular works including biographies, commentaries, basic doctrine and Christian living. Our children's books are also published in this imprint.

Mentor focuses on books written at a level suitable for Bible College and seminary students, pastors, and other serious readers. The imprint includes commentaries, doctrinal studies, examination of current issues and church history.

Christian Heritage contains classic writings from the past.

Christian Focus Publications Ltd
Geanies House, Fearn,
Ross-shire, IV20 1TW, Scotland, United Kingdom
info@christianfocus.com

Our titles are available from quality bookstores and
www.christianfocus.com